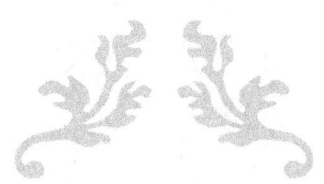

ADULTS COLORING PAGES

STRESS RELIEVE PATTERN

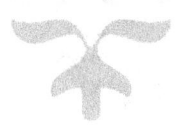

NOVEMBER 19, 2018
AUTHOR – SADDAM NA
NEW DELHI -

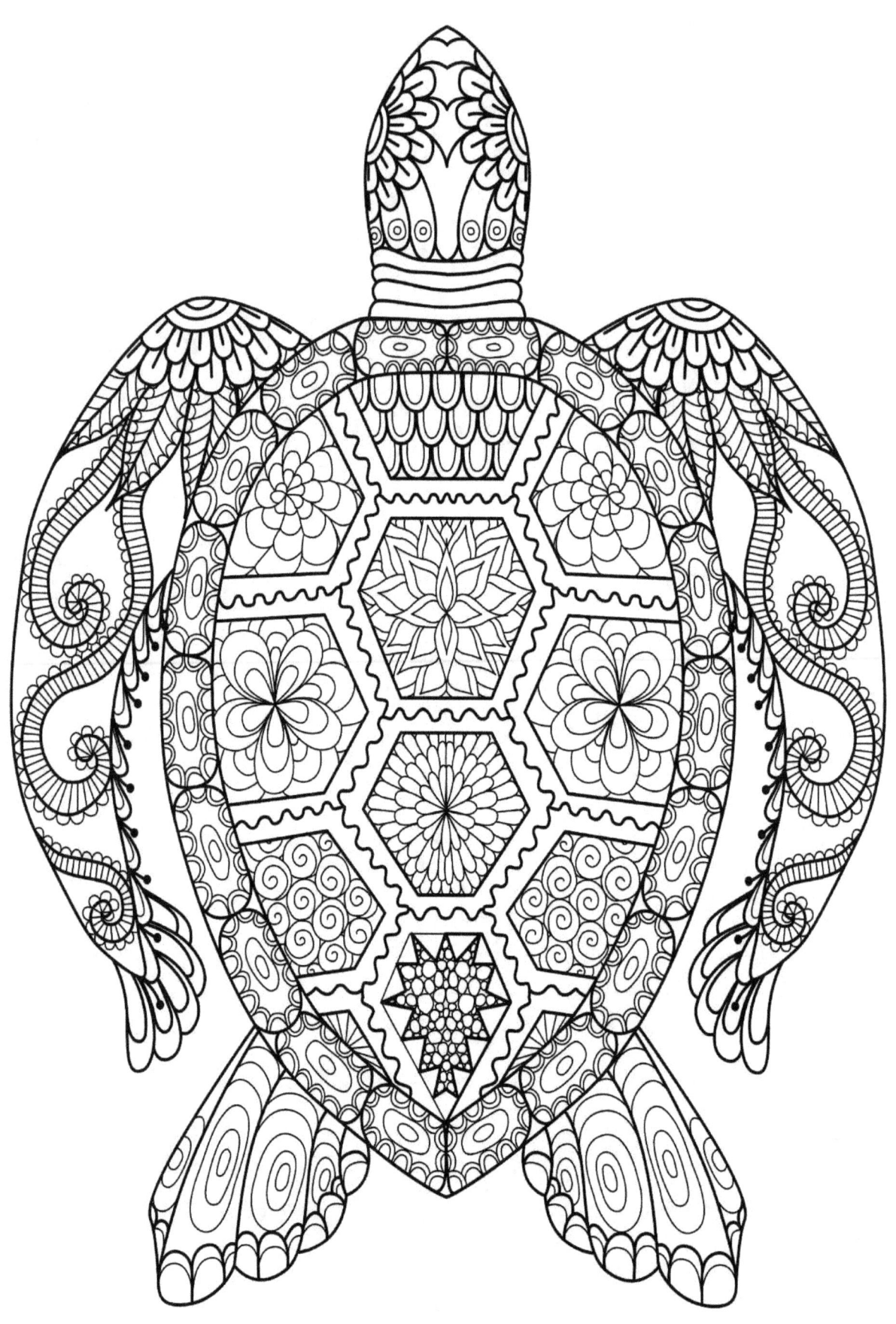

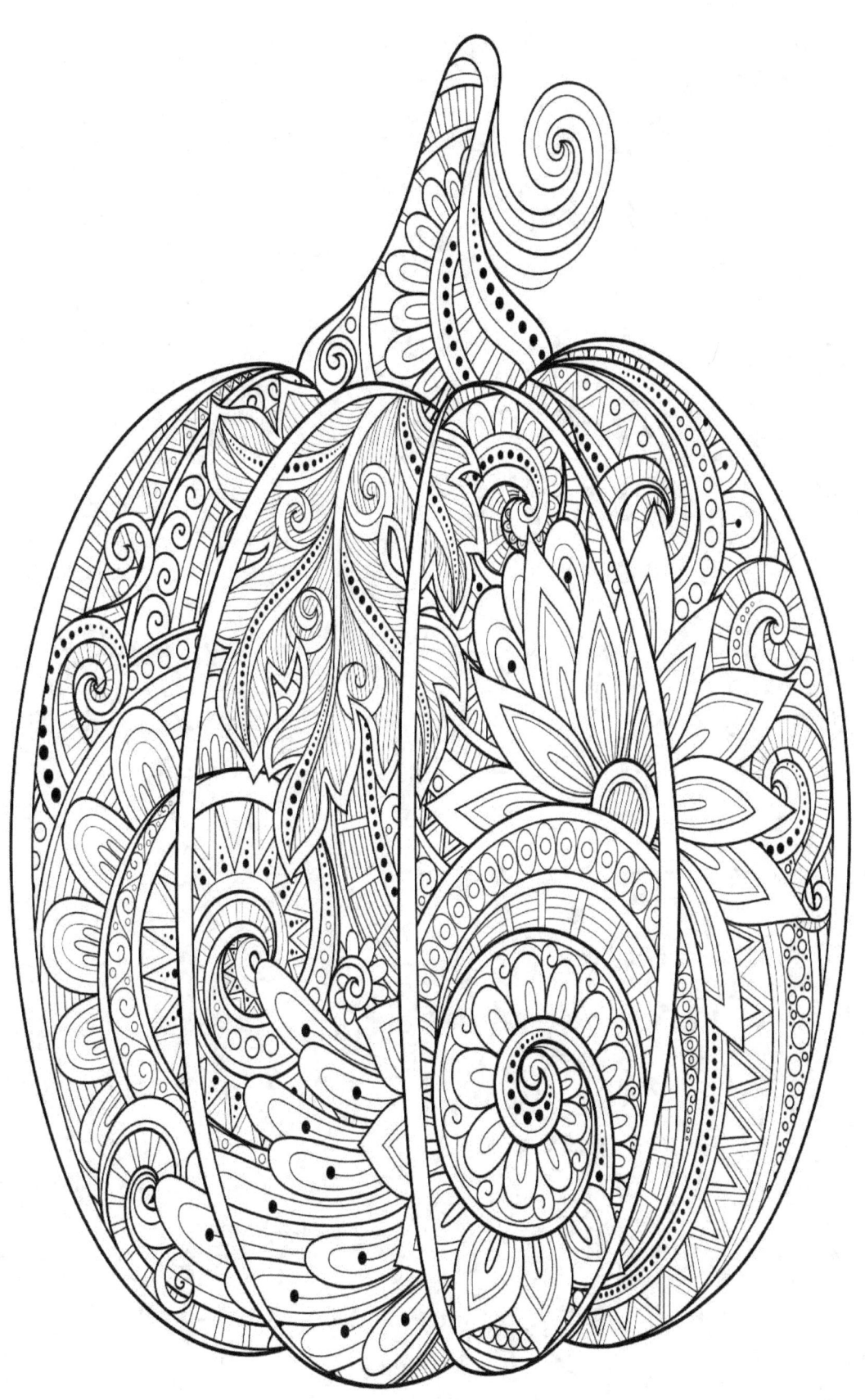

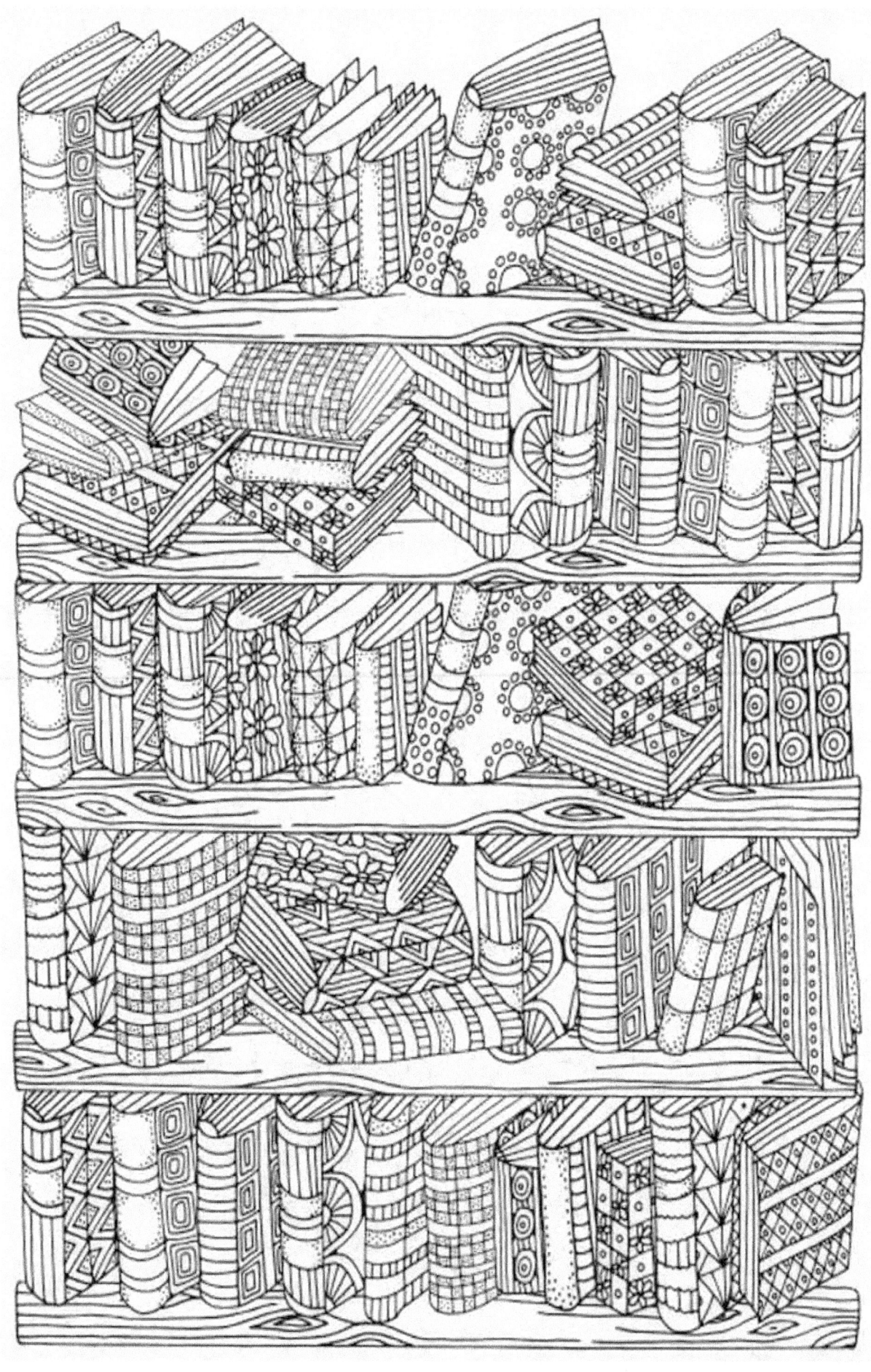

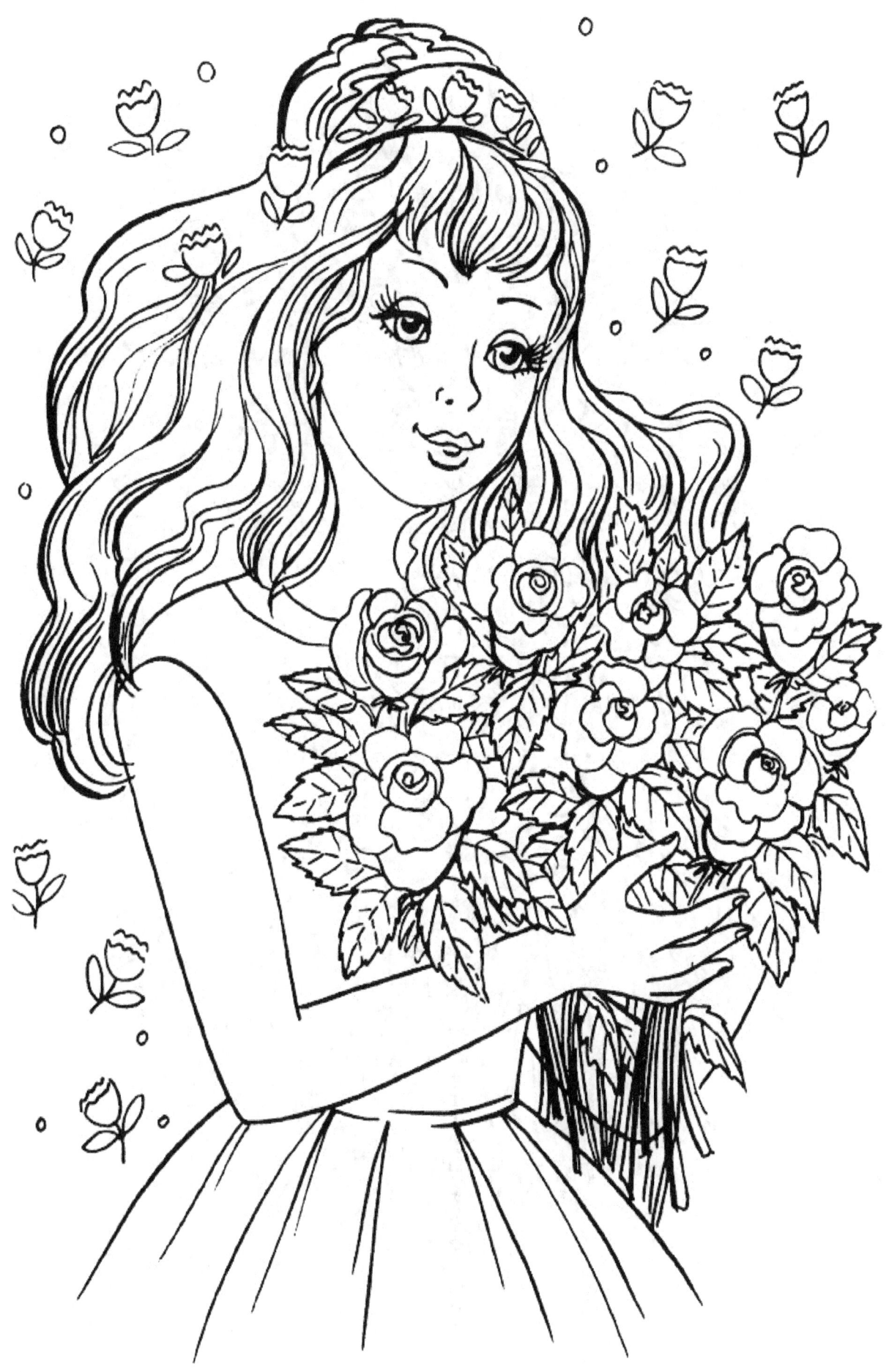

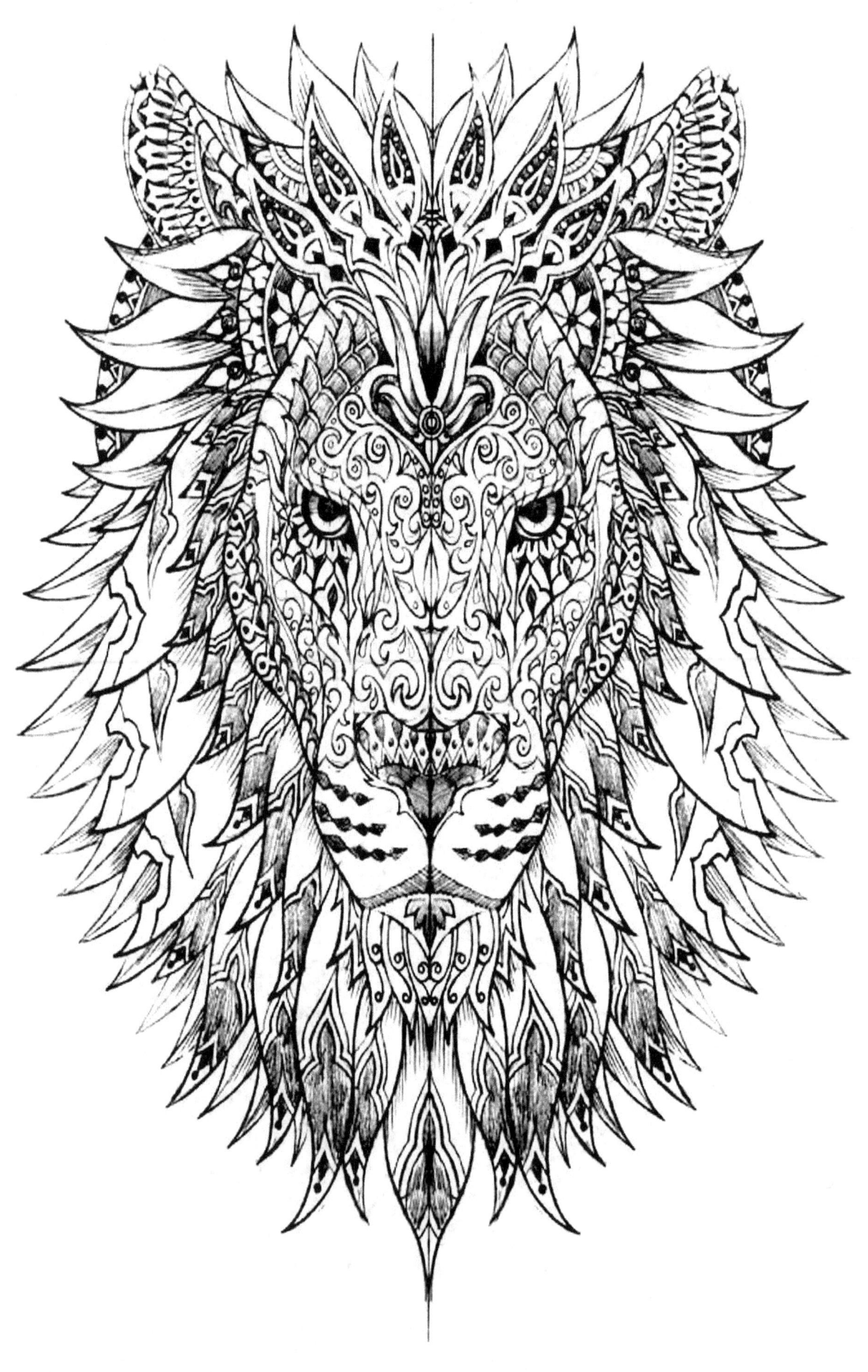

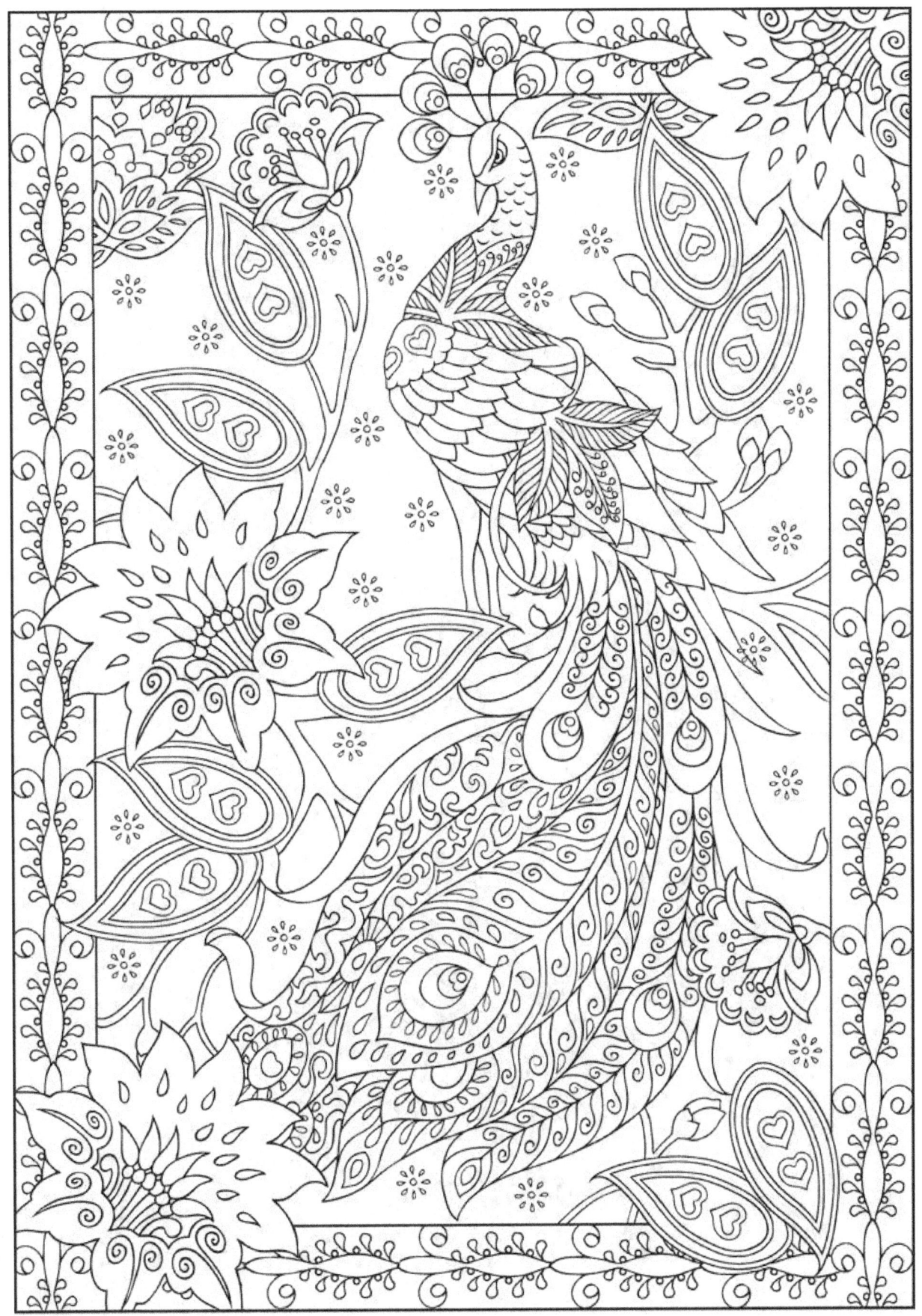

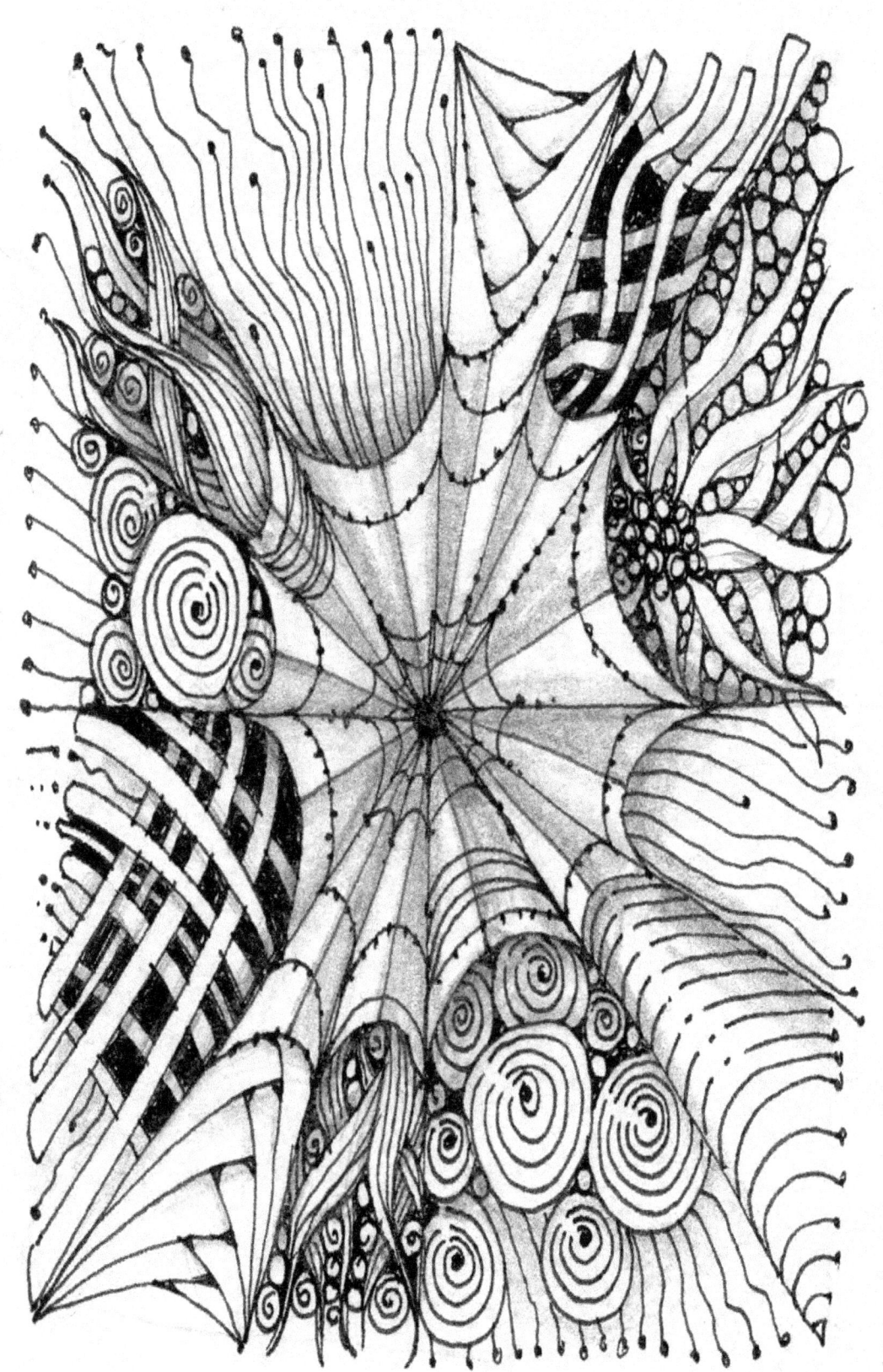

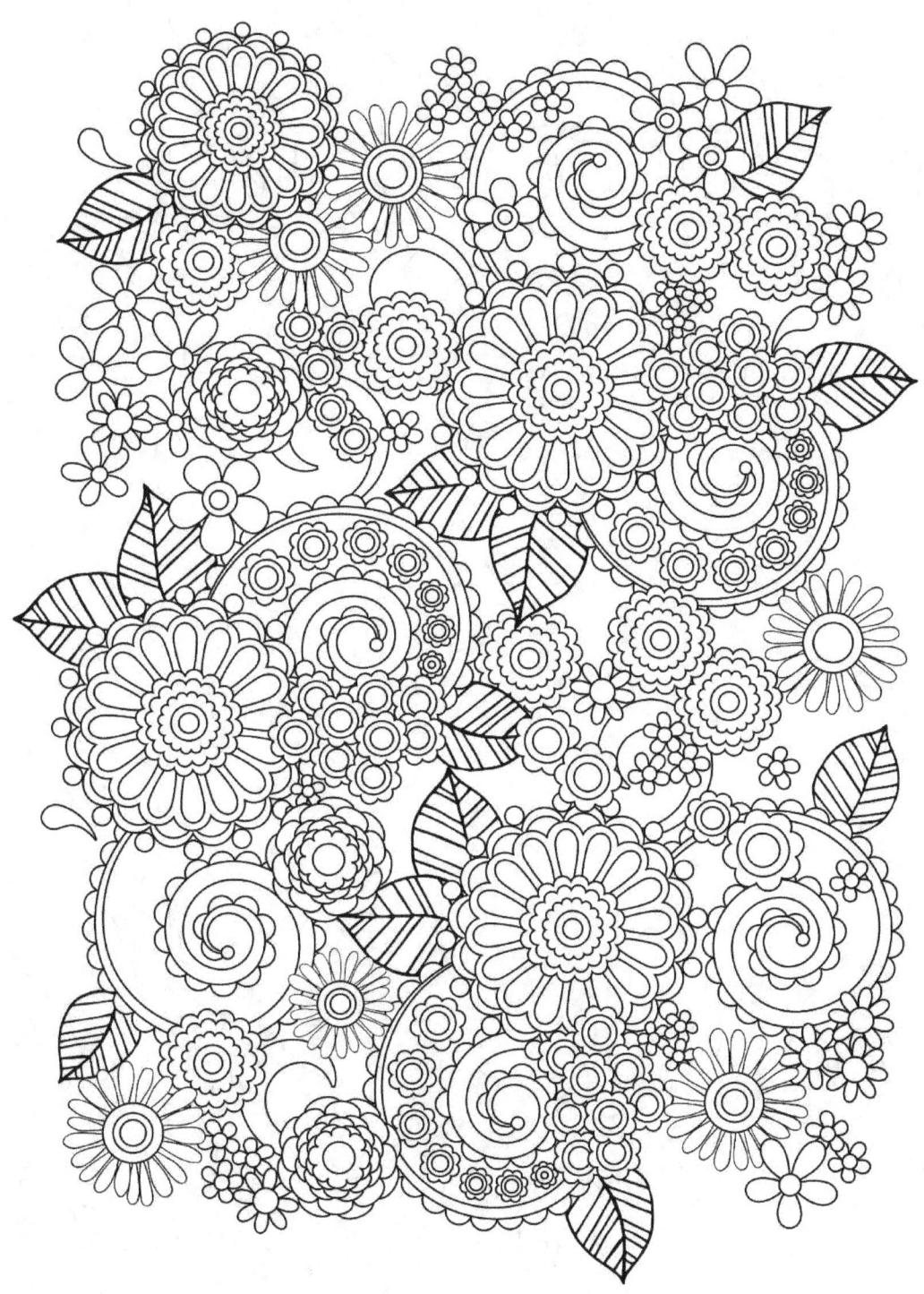

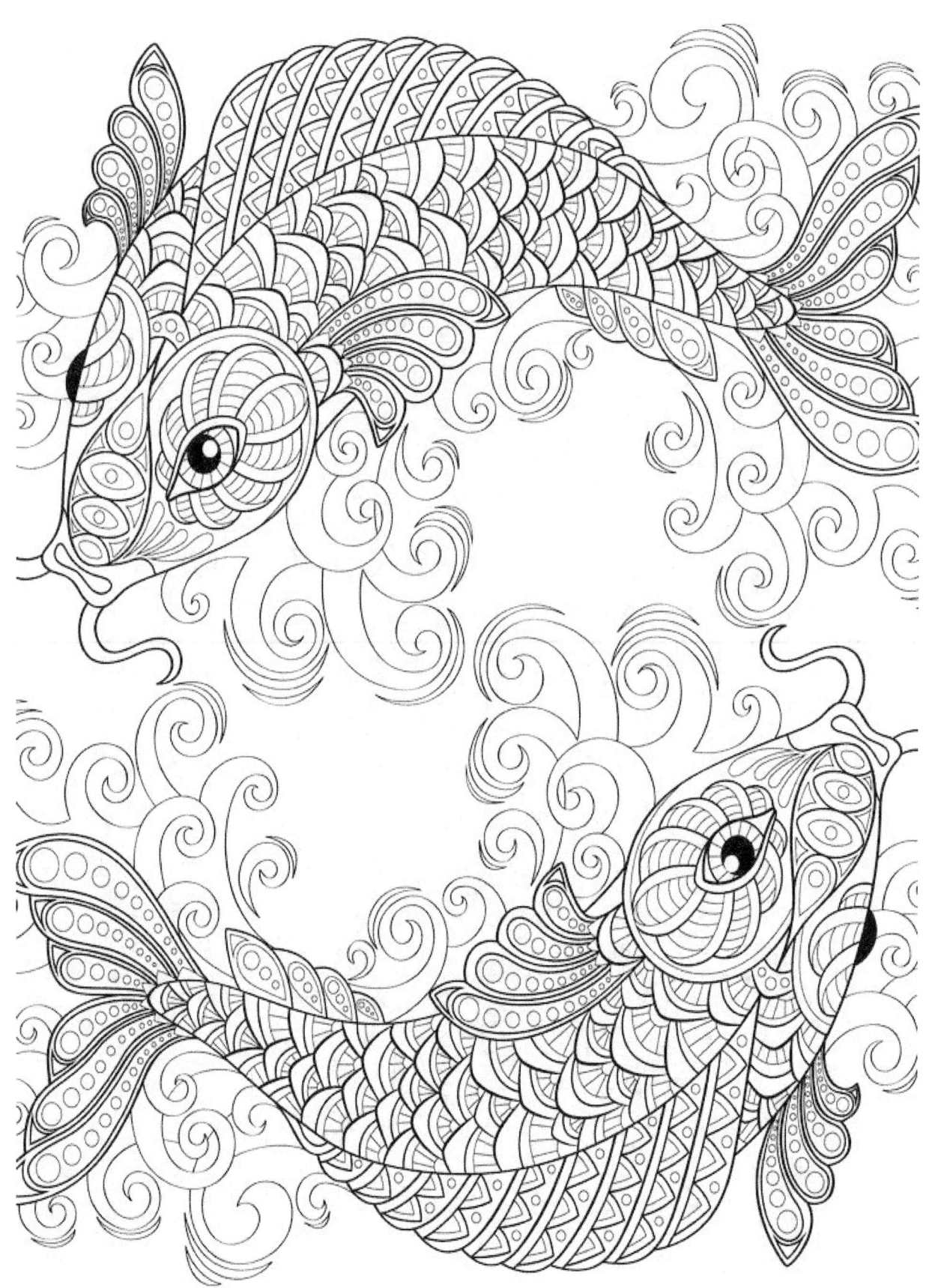

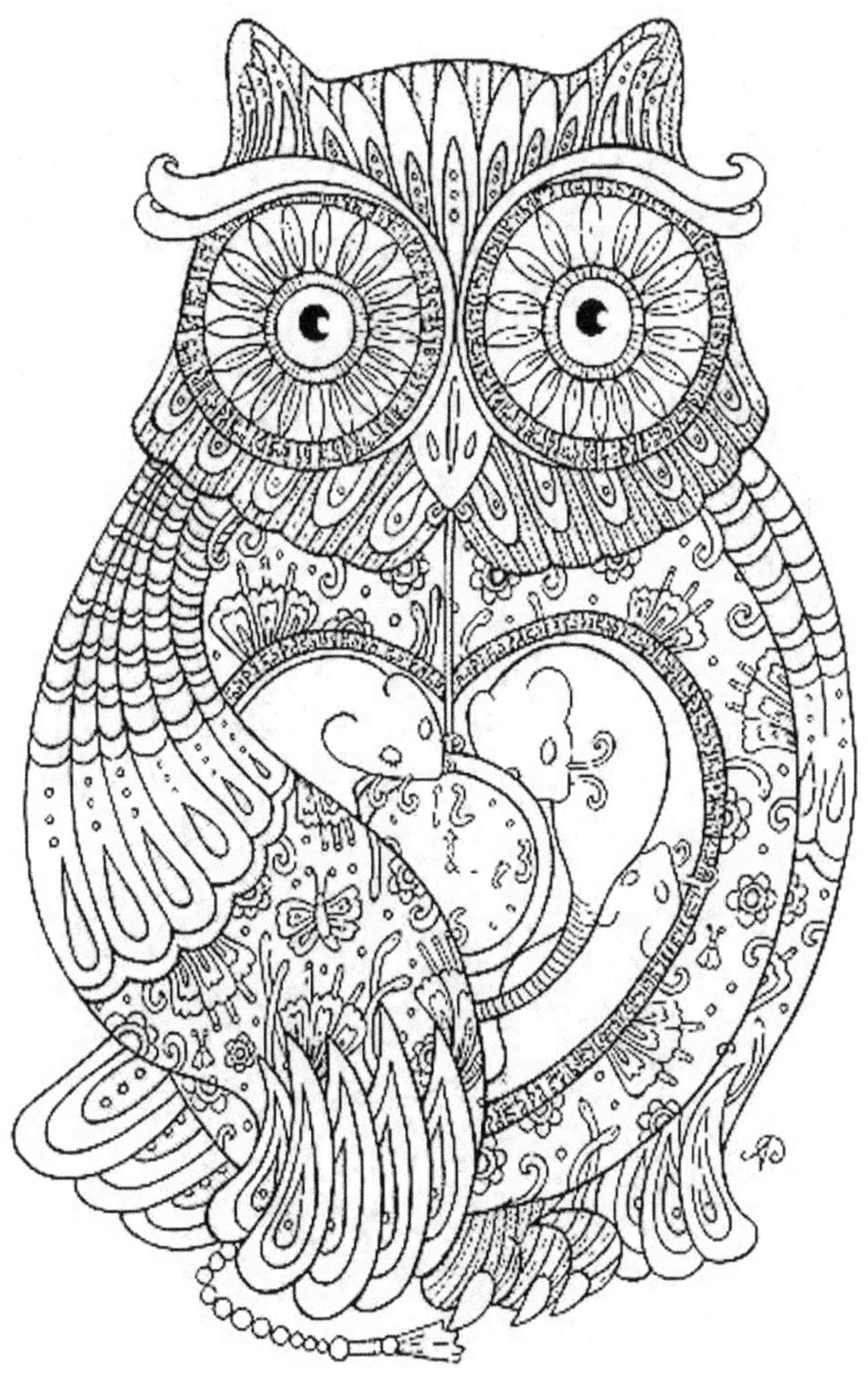

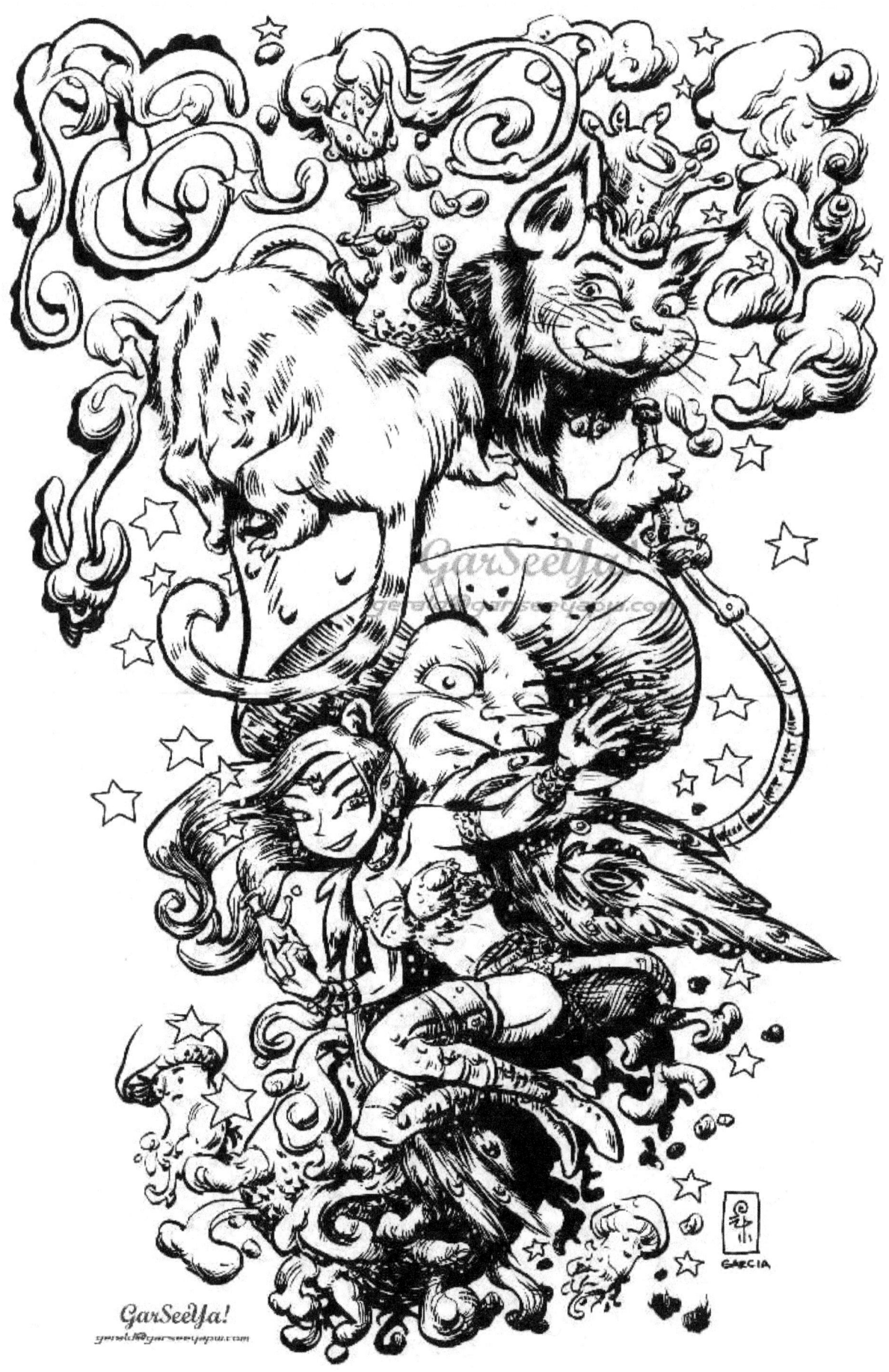

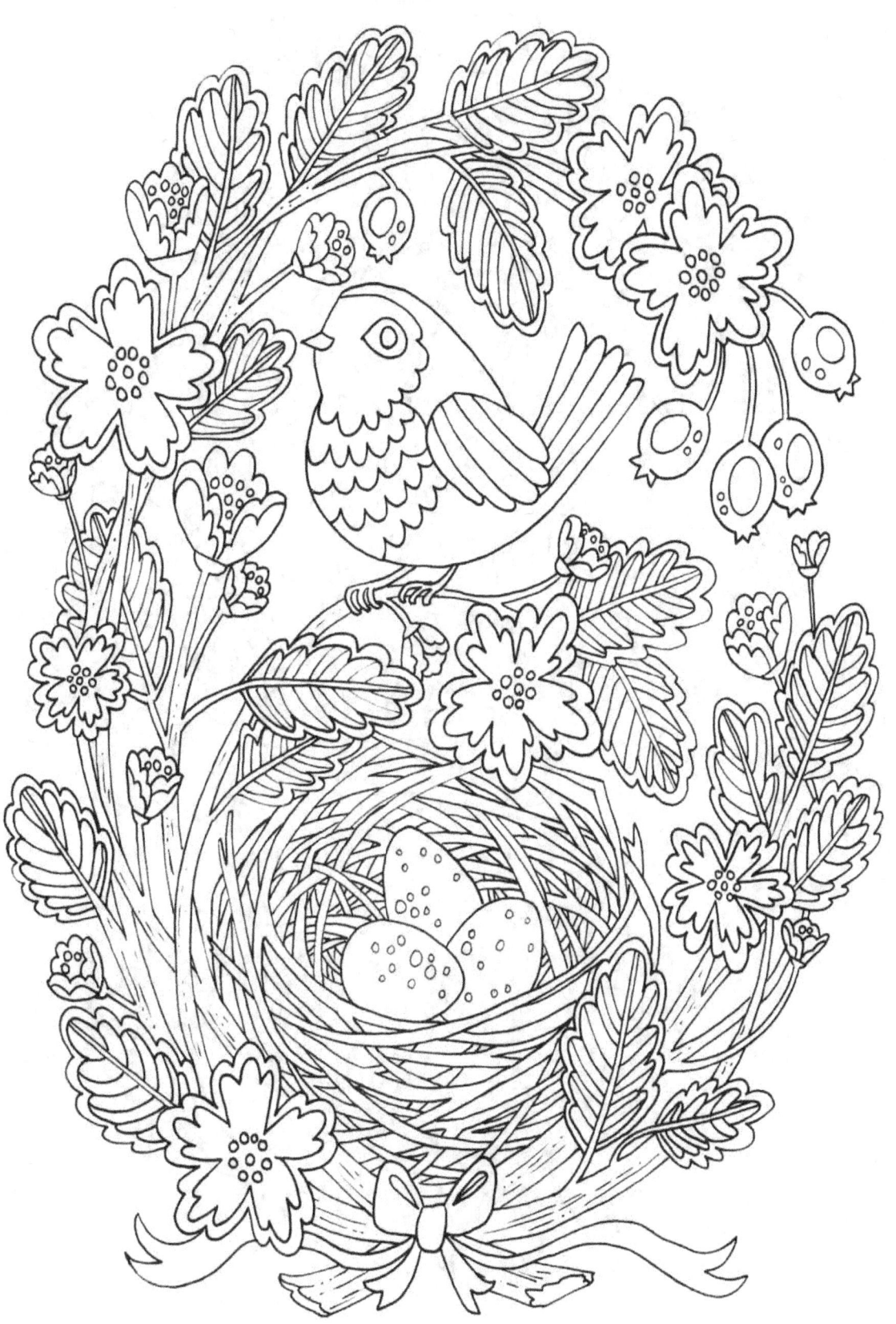

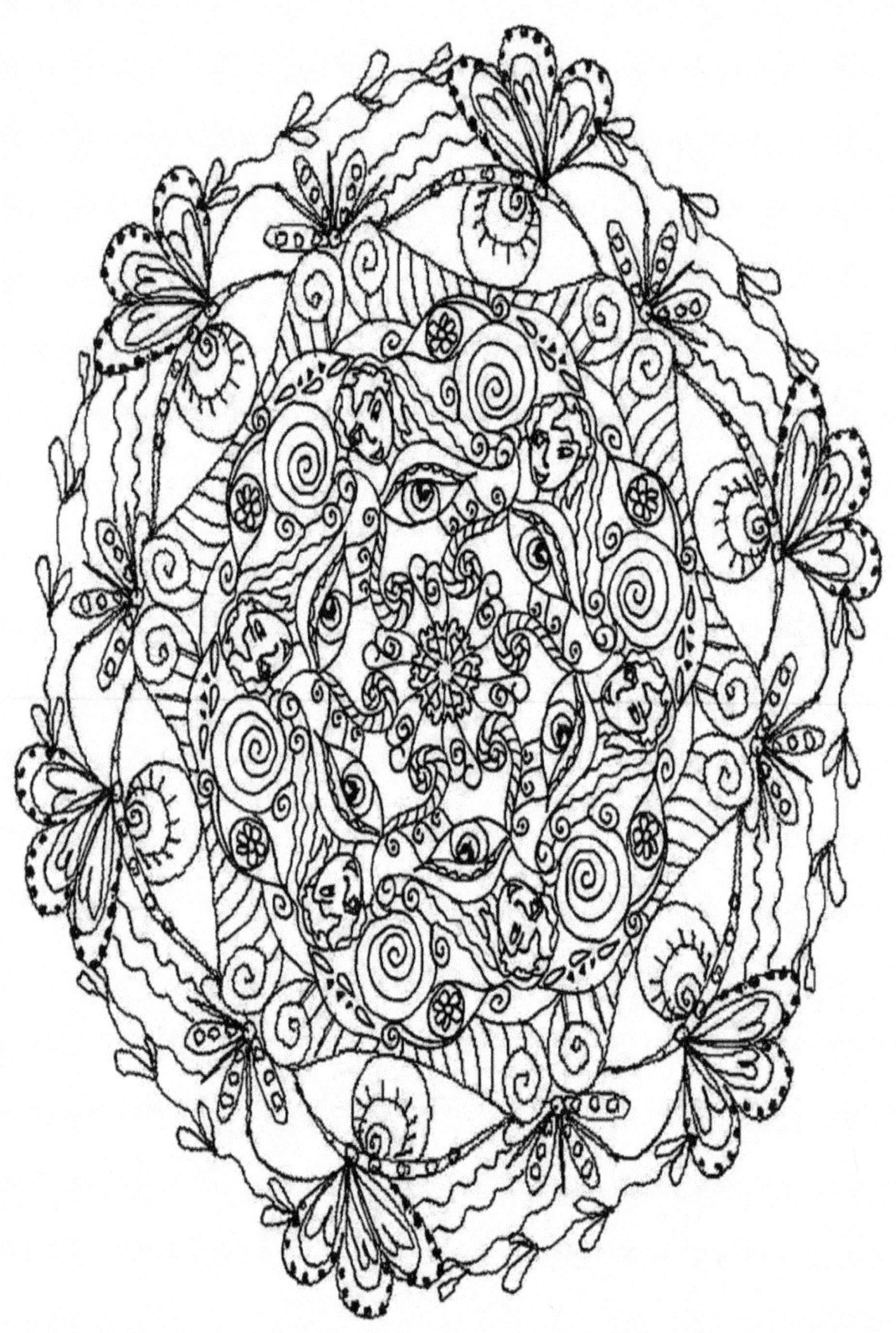

www.Milliande.com

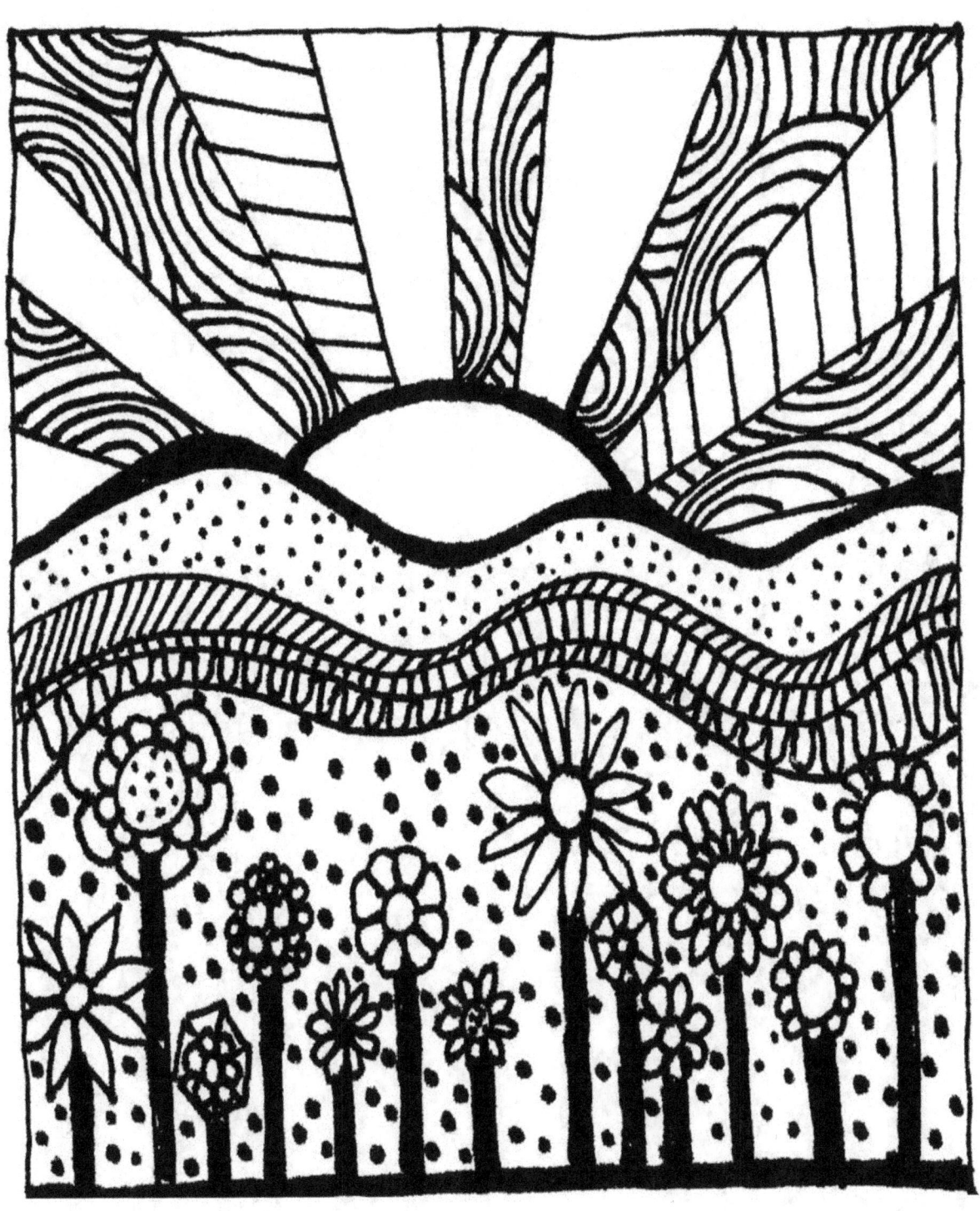

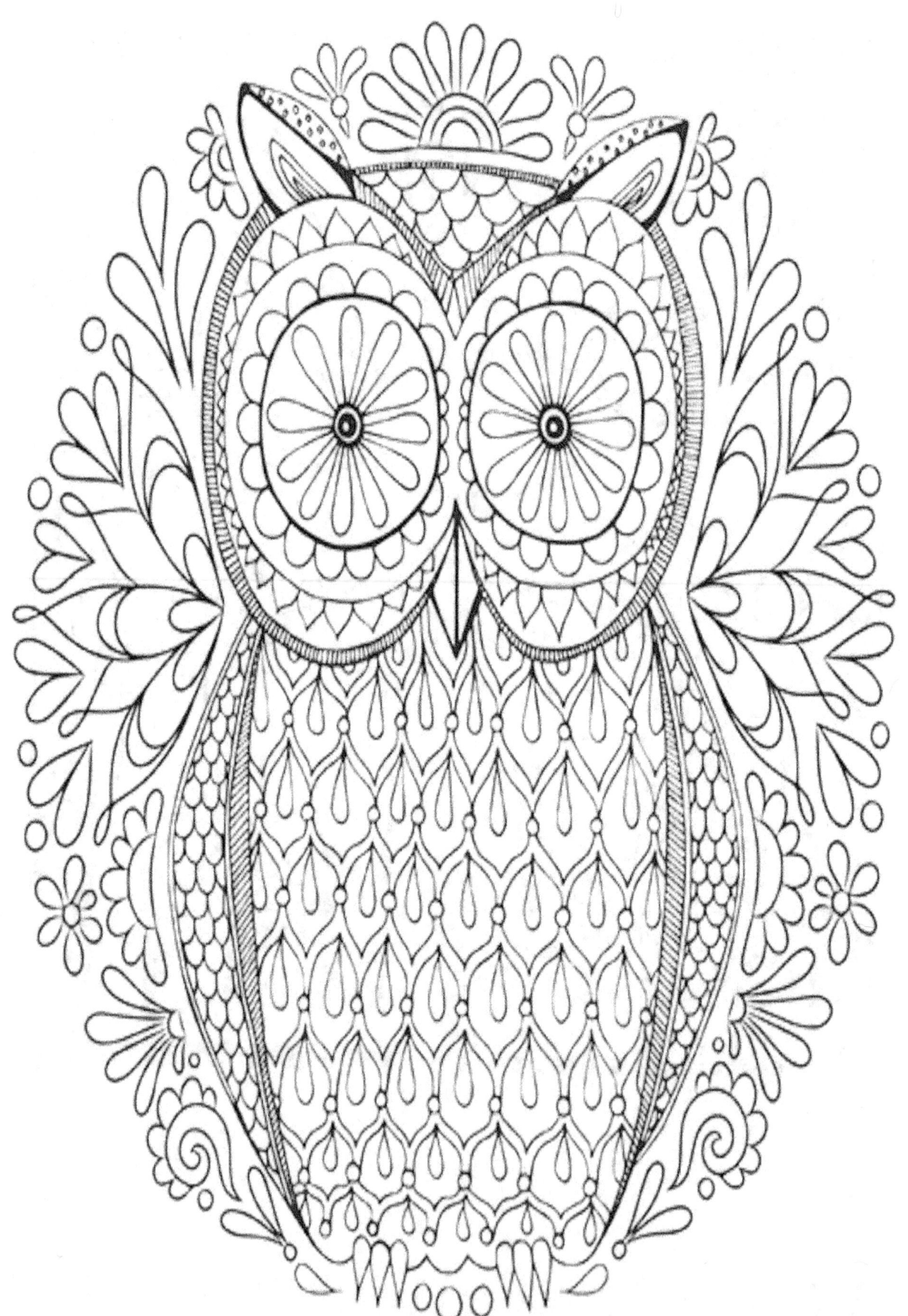

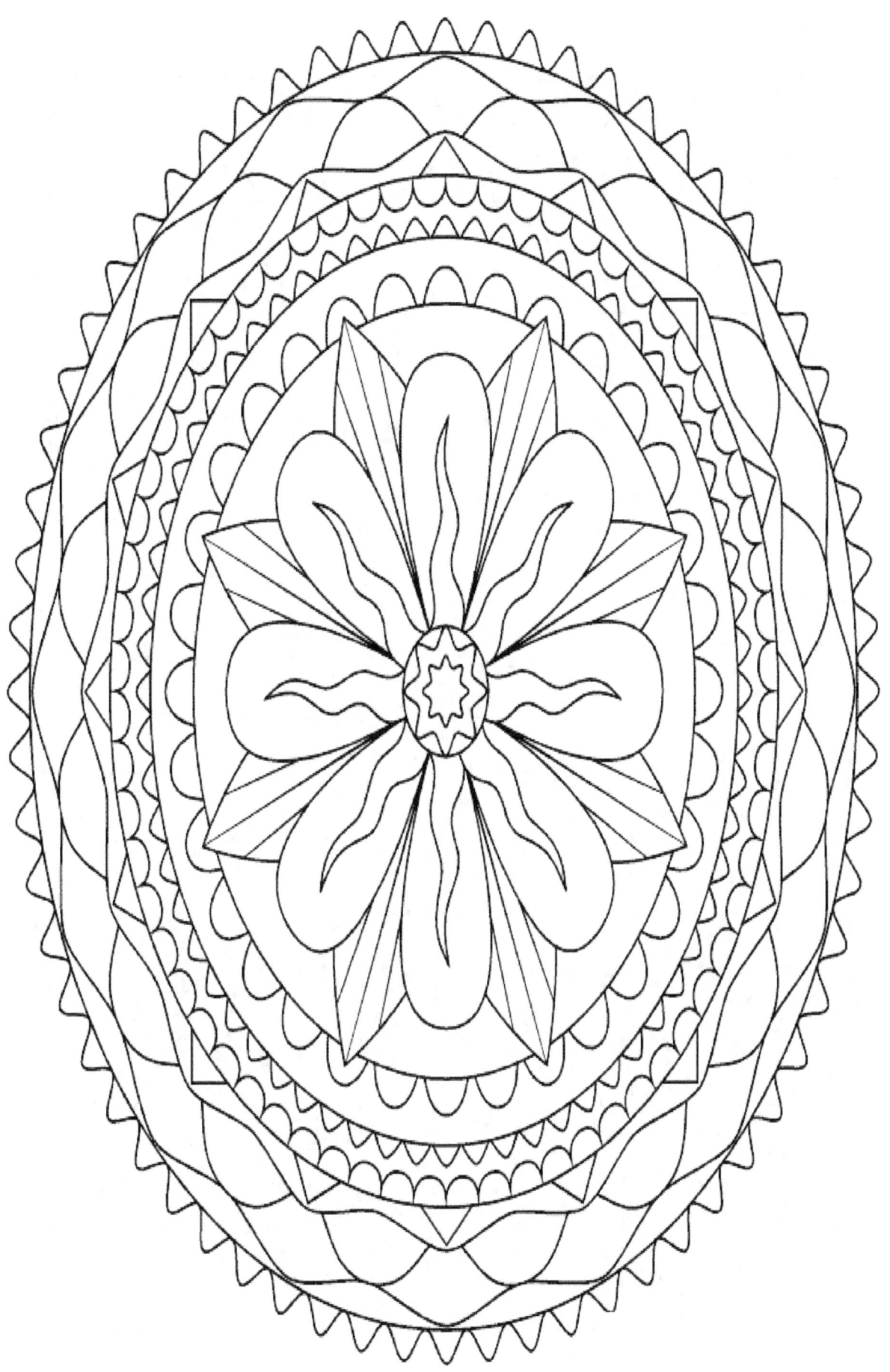

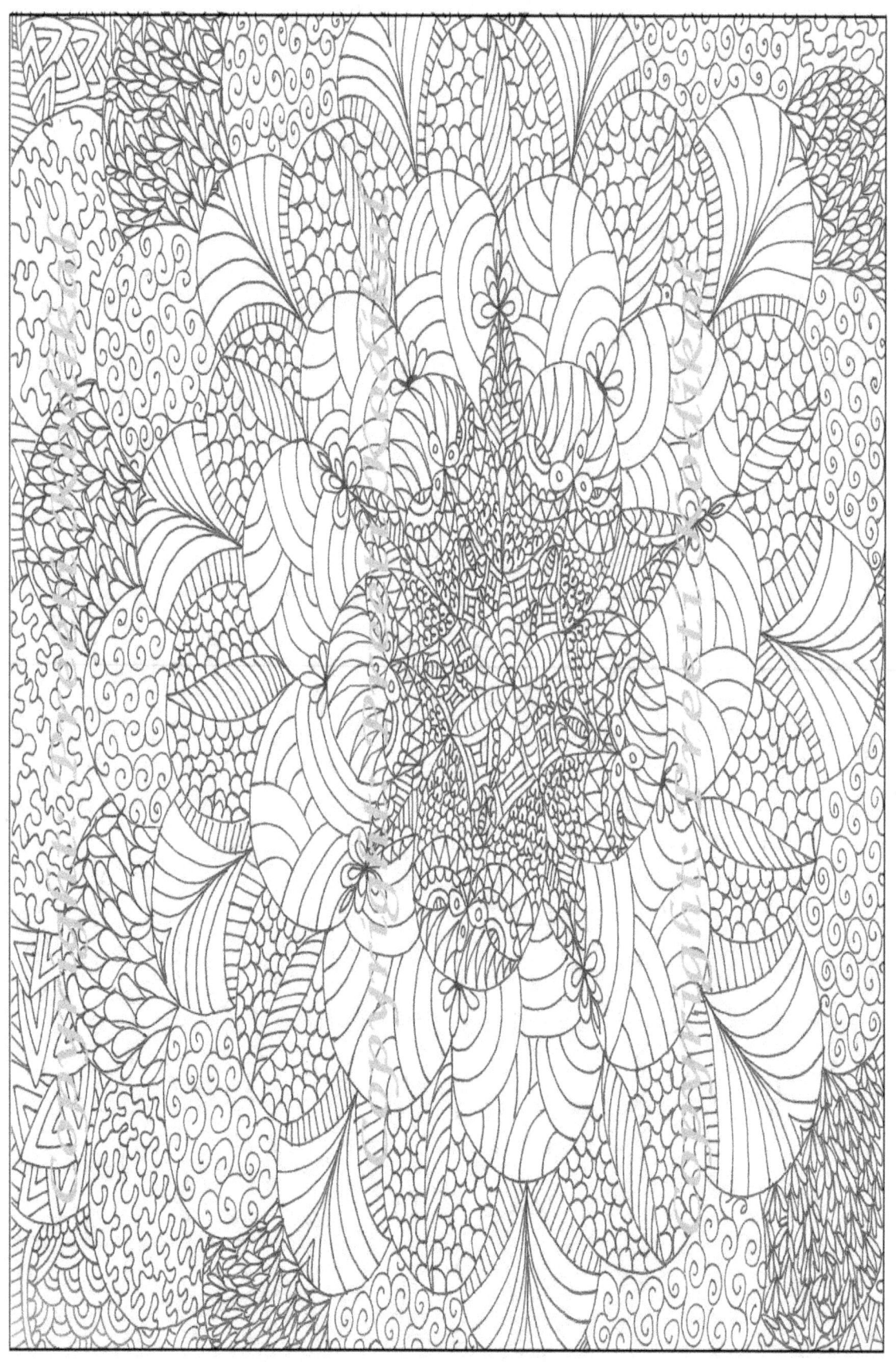

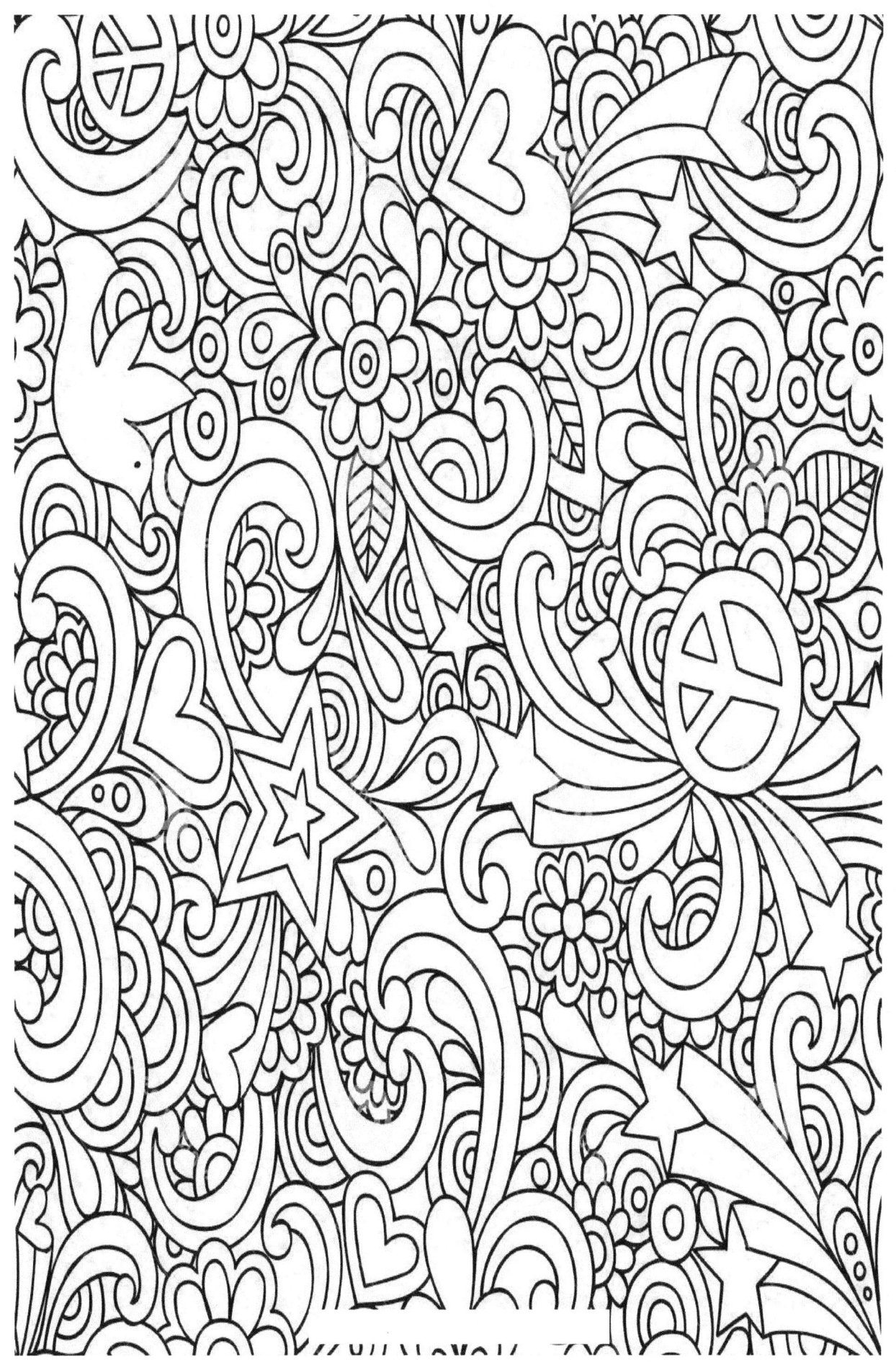

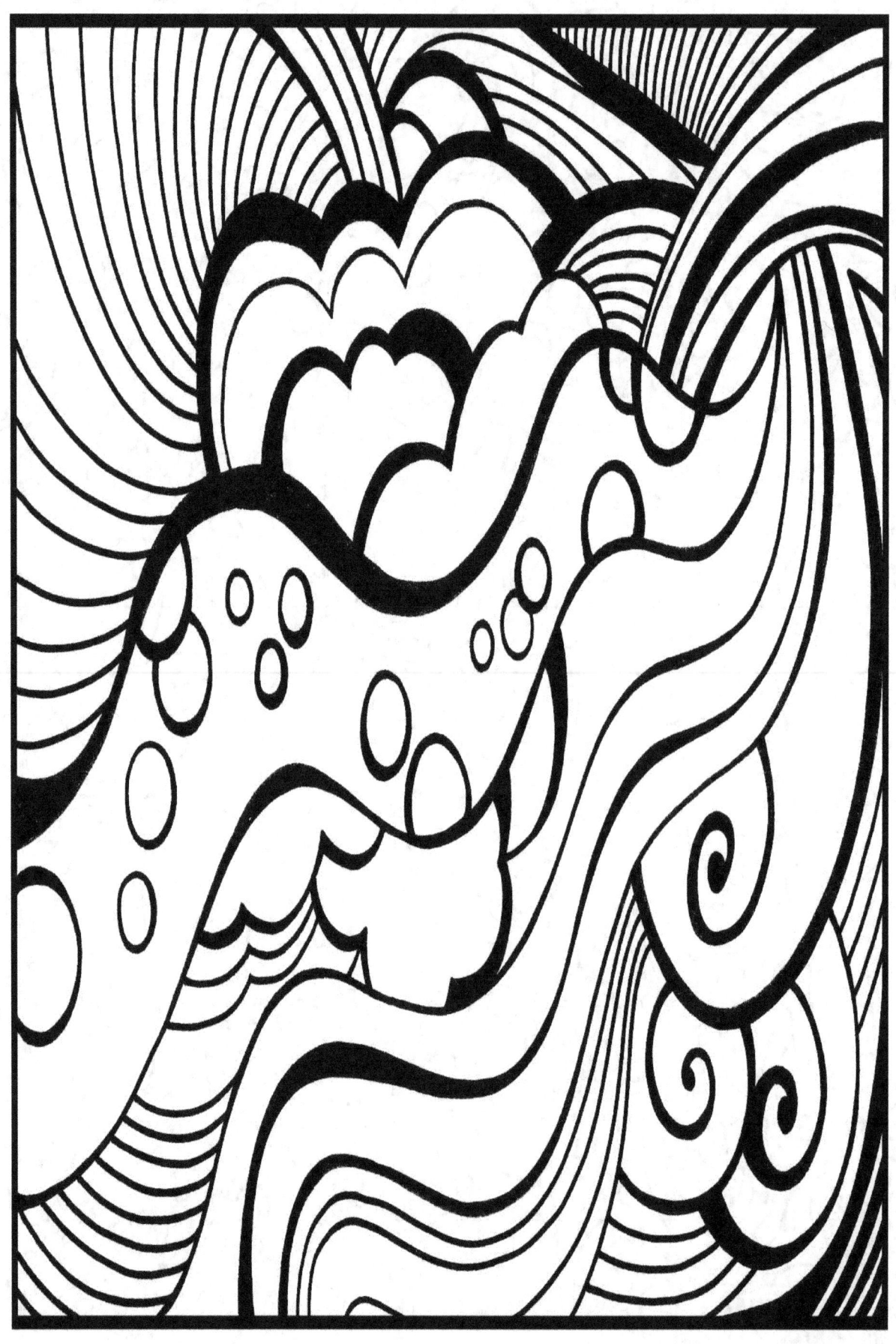

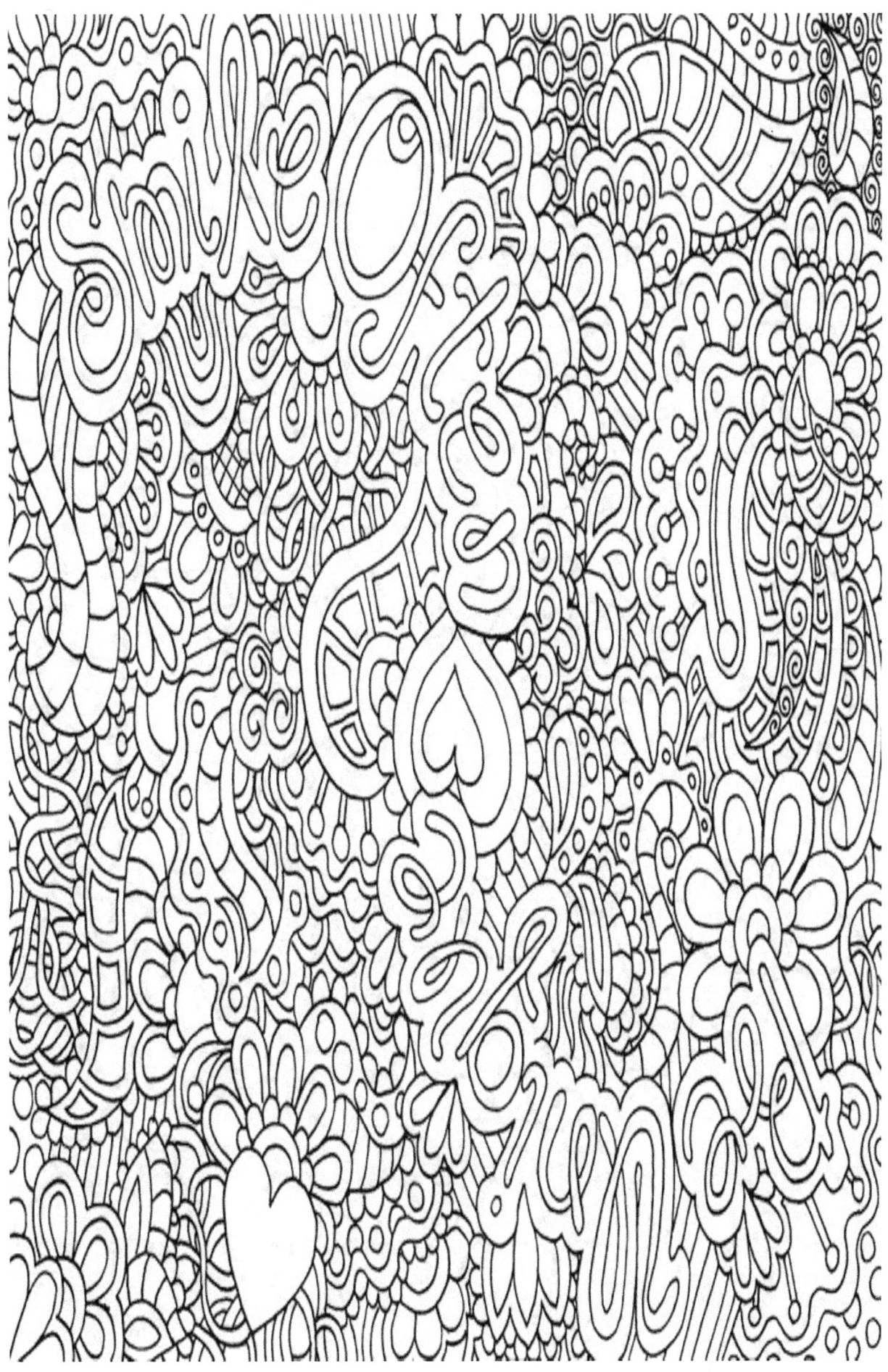

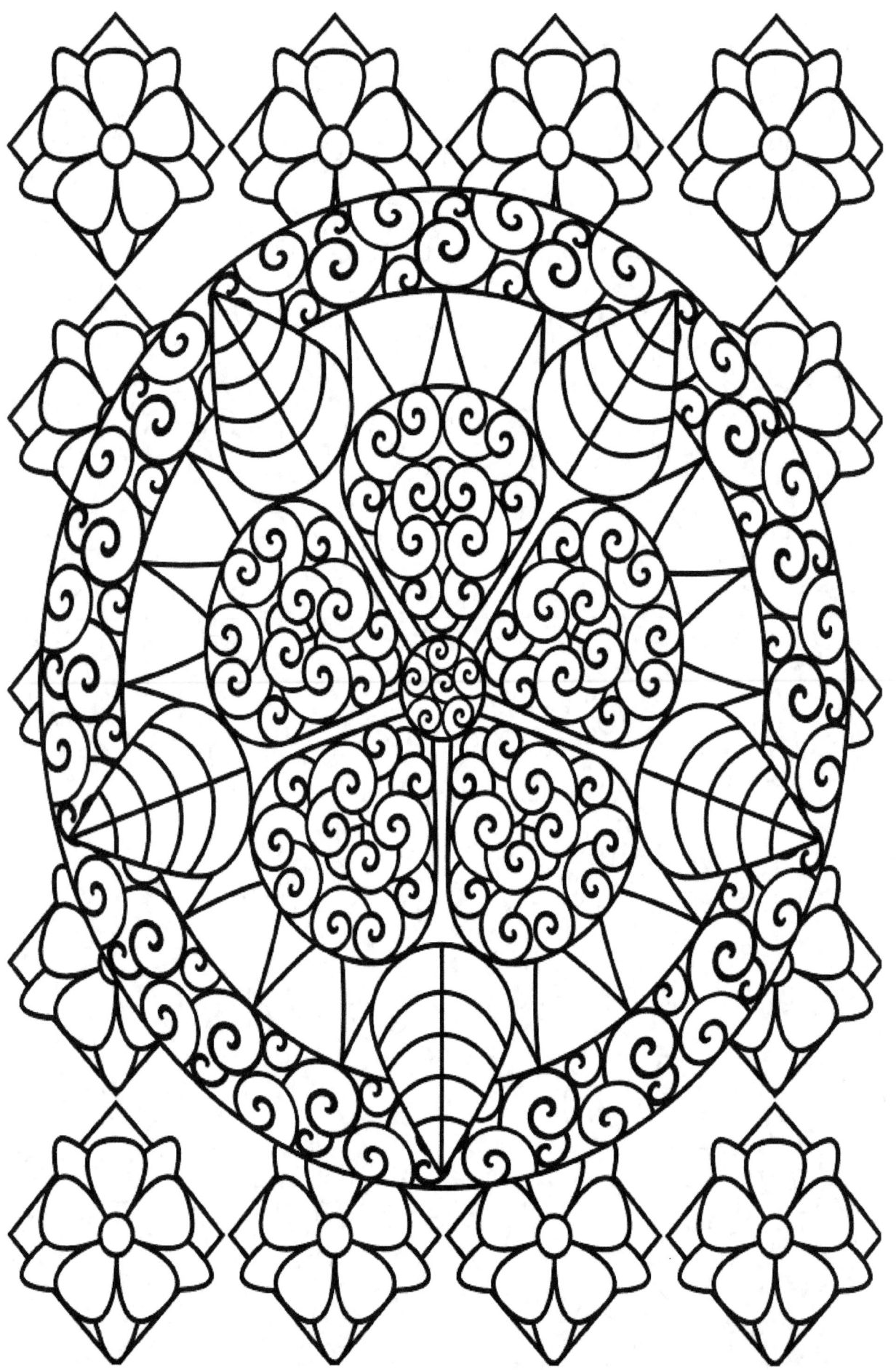

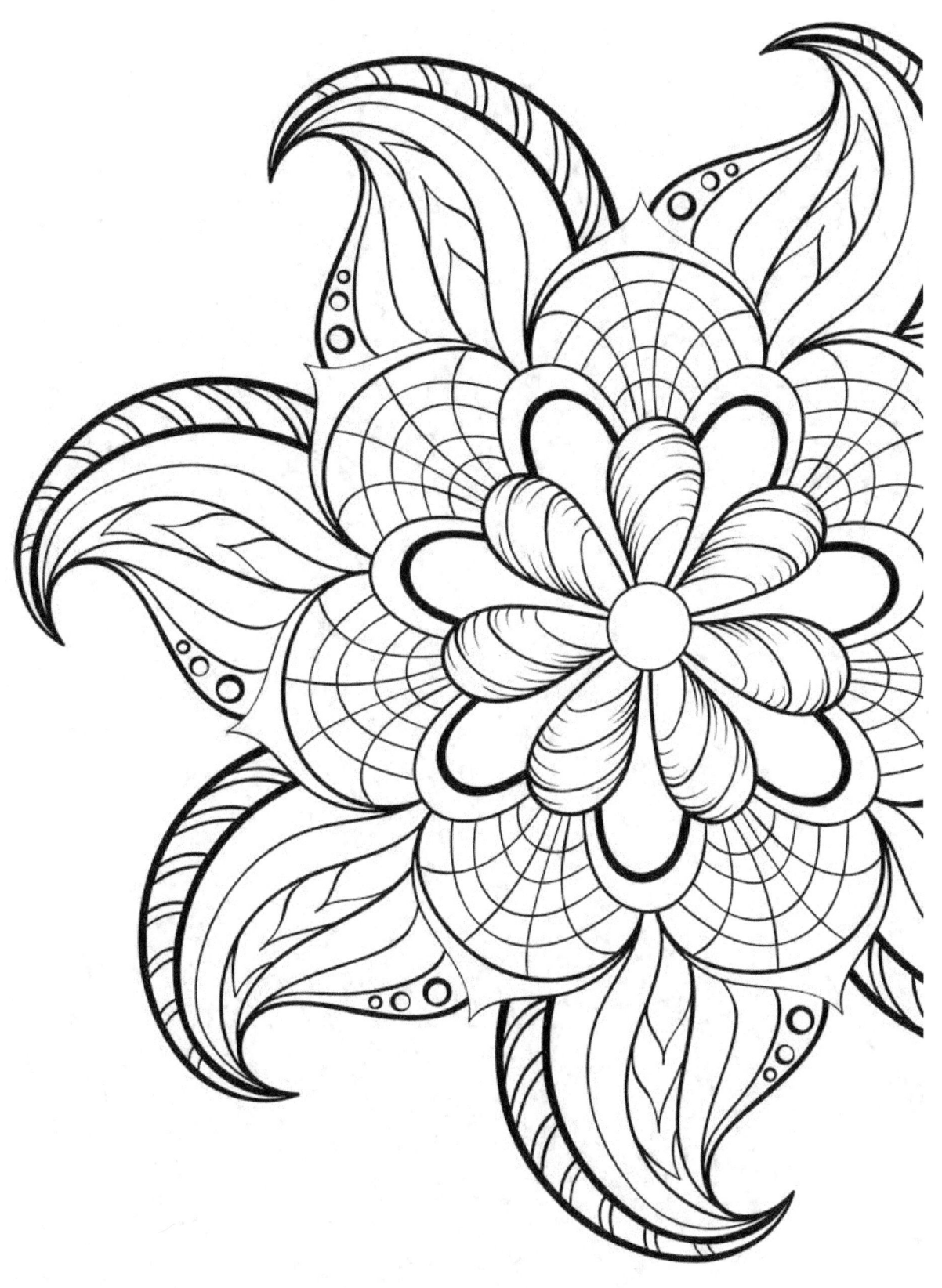

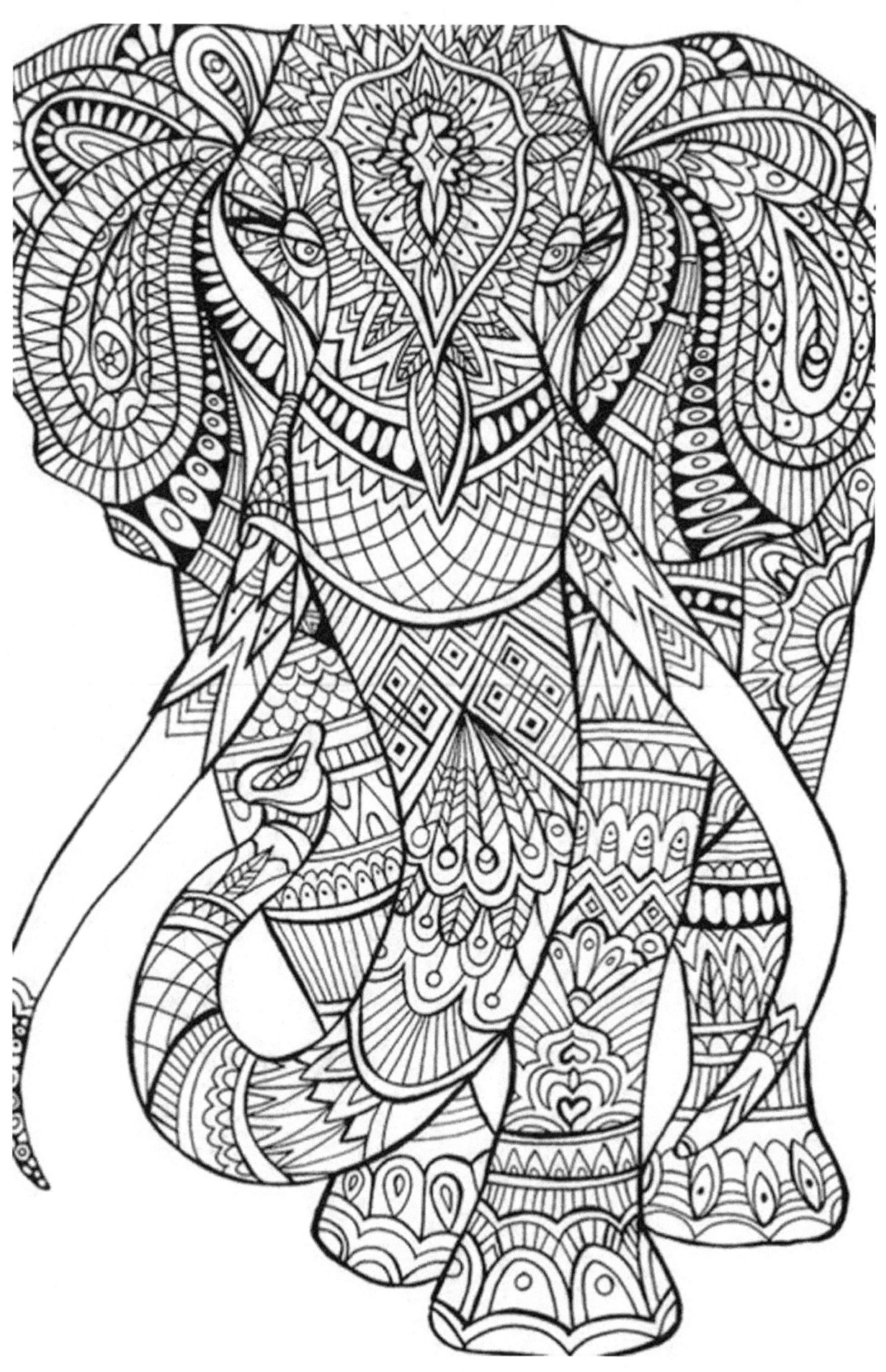

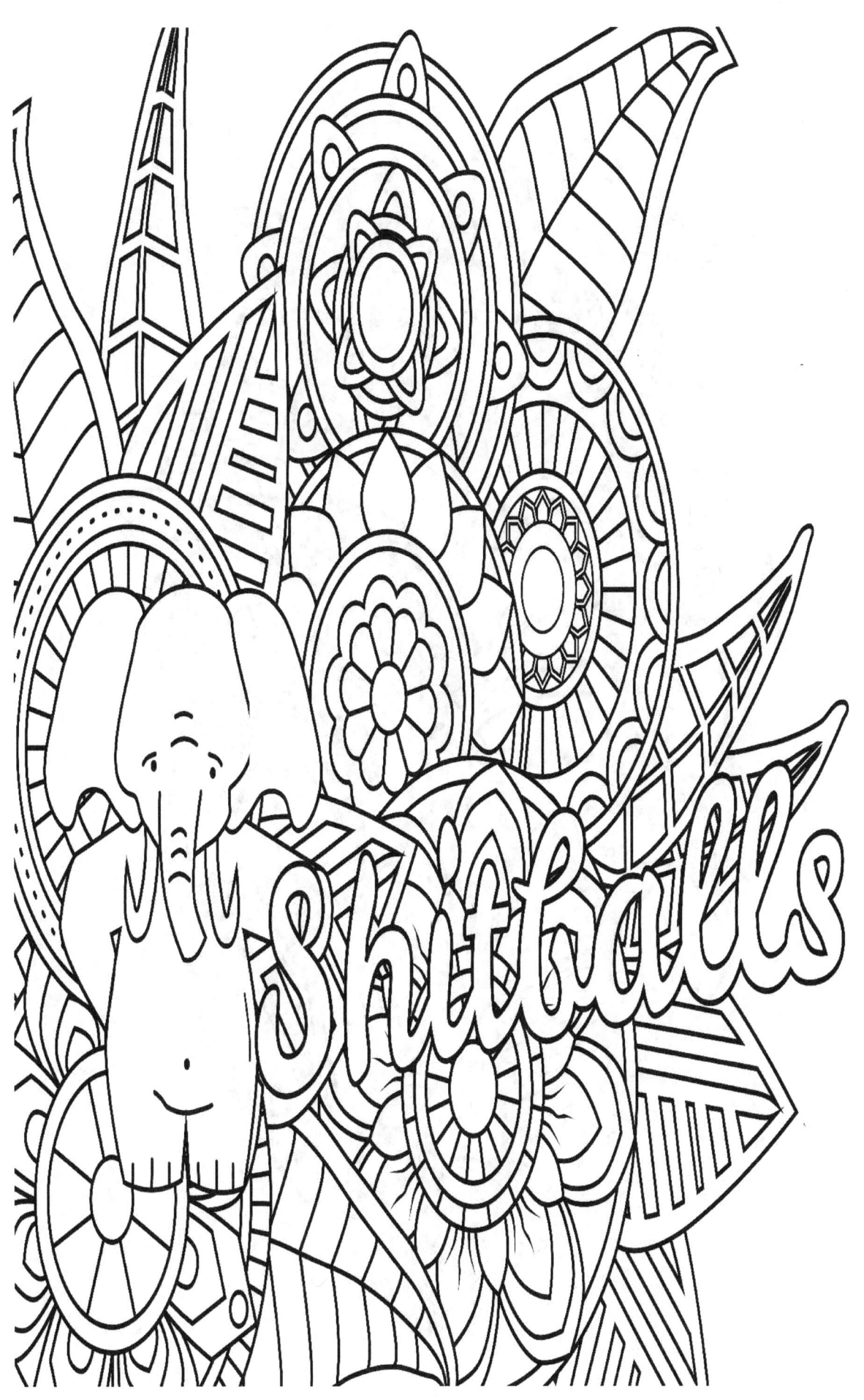

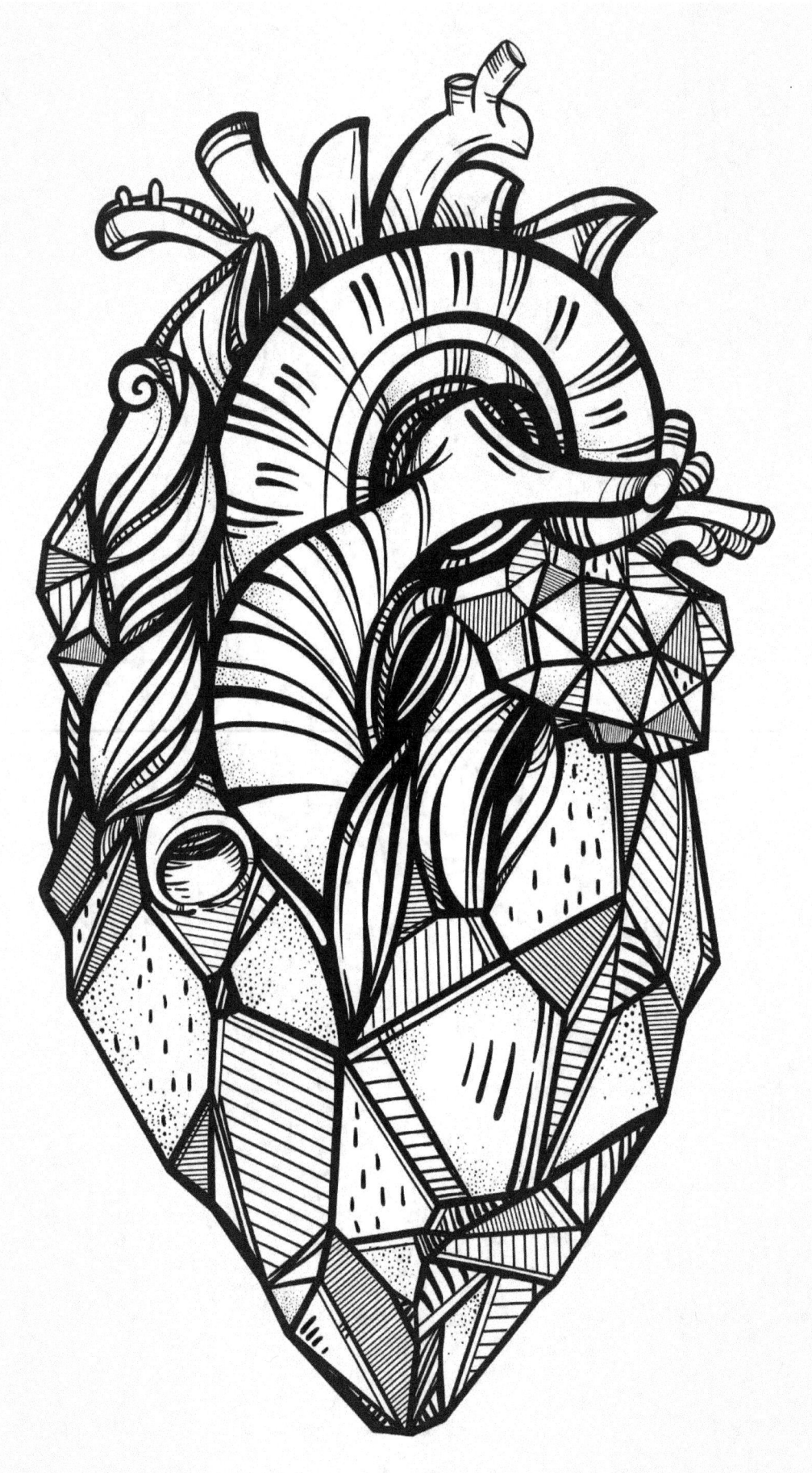

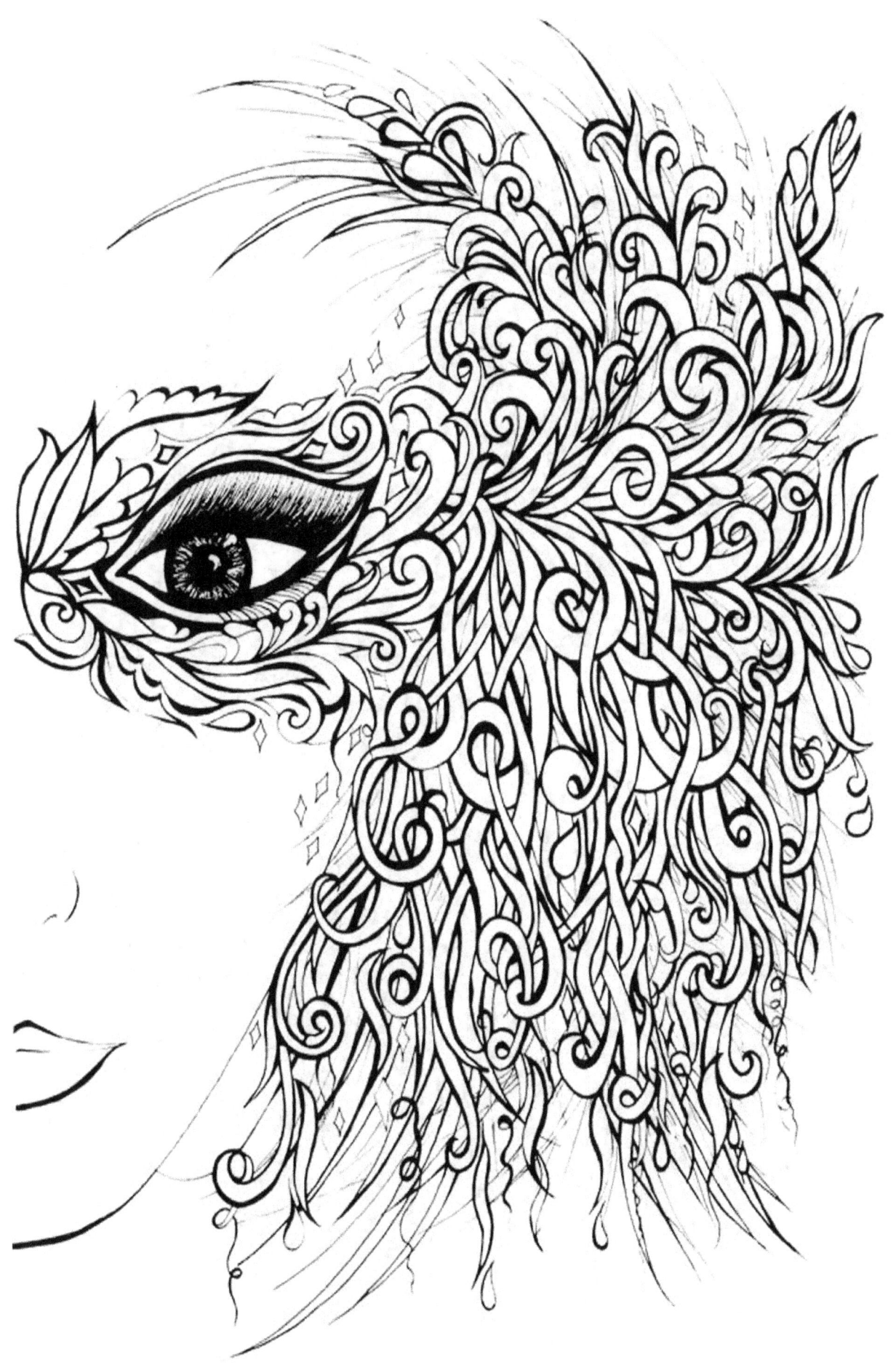

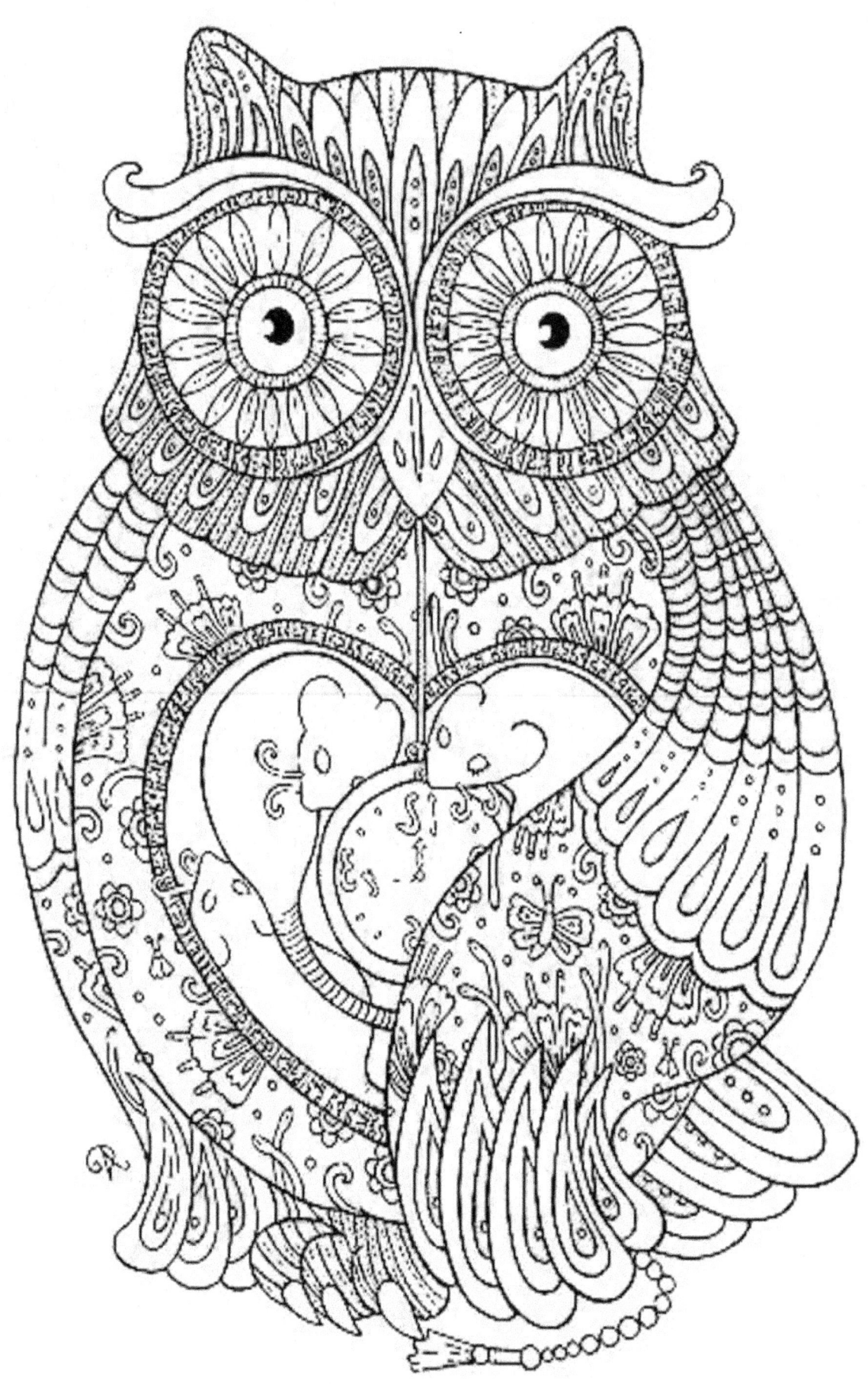

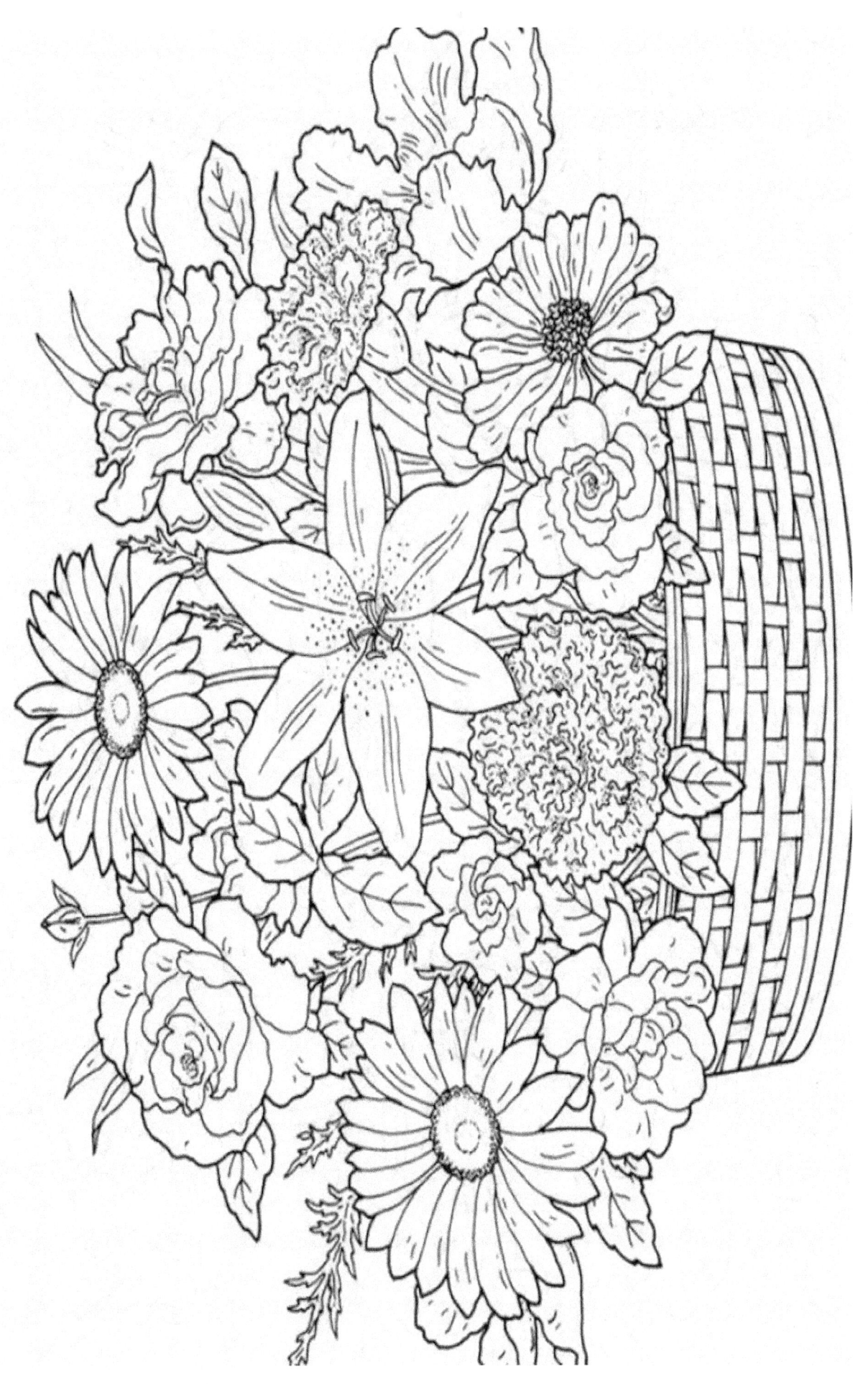

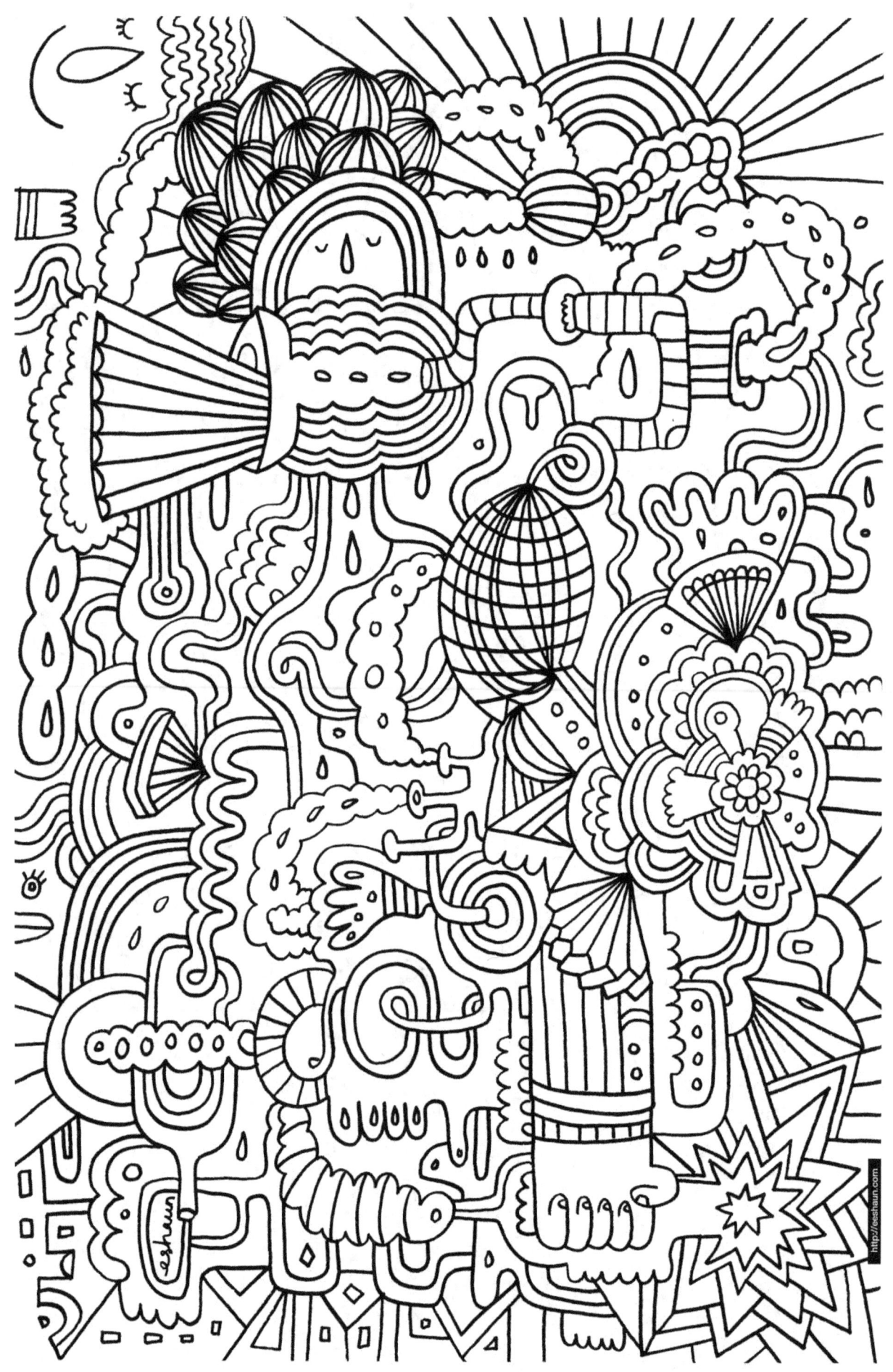

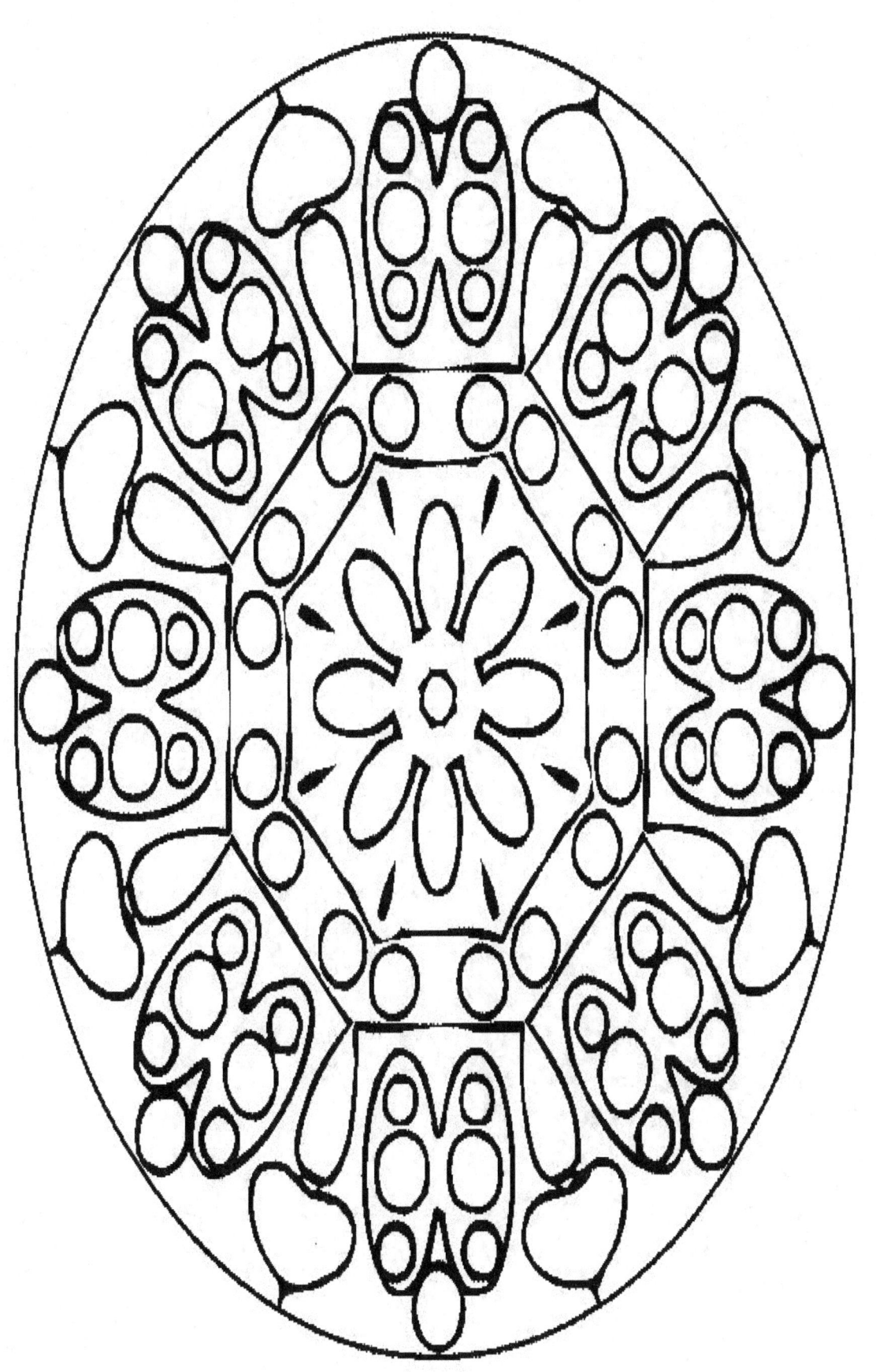

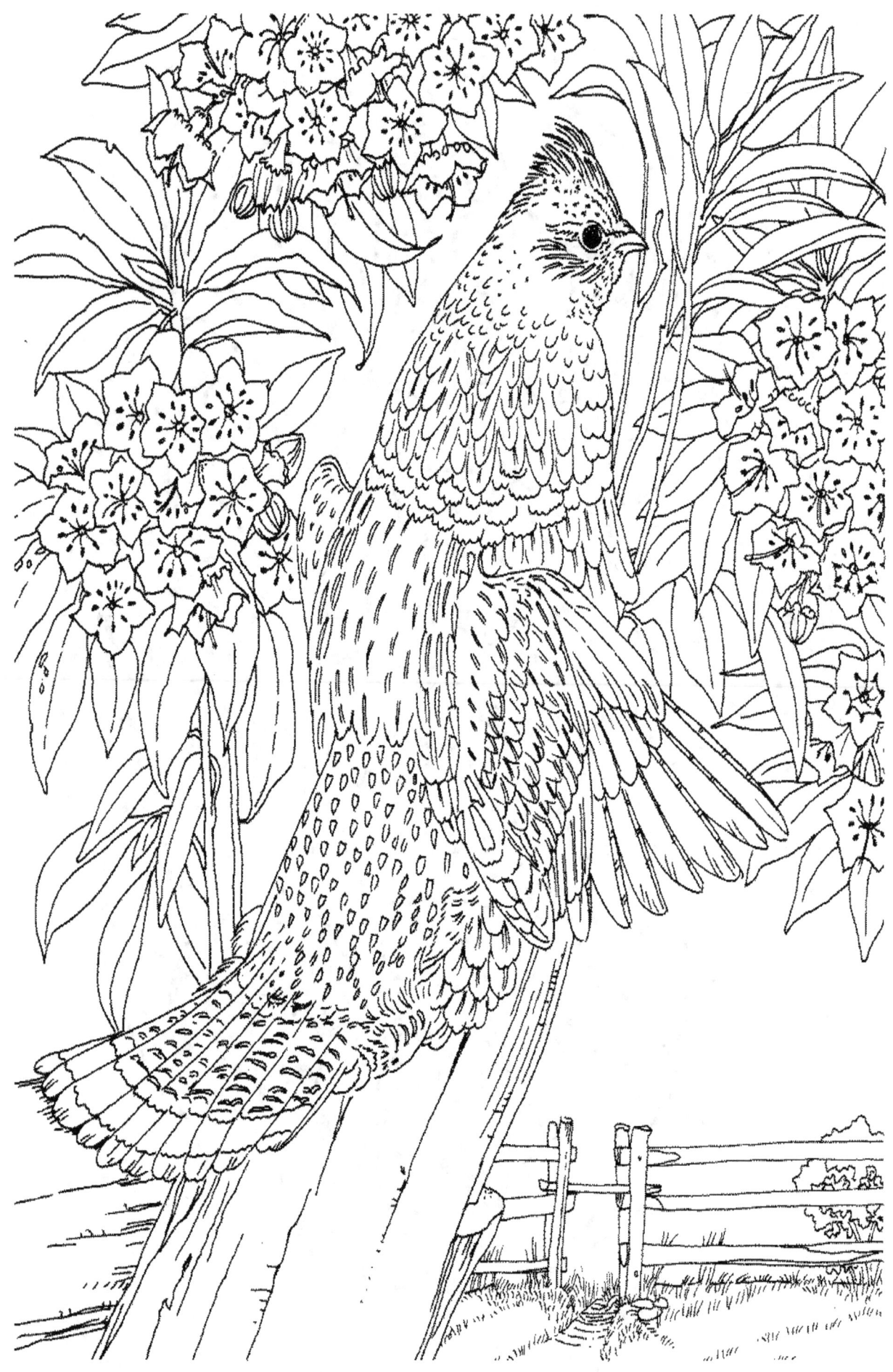

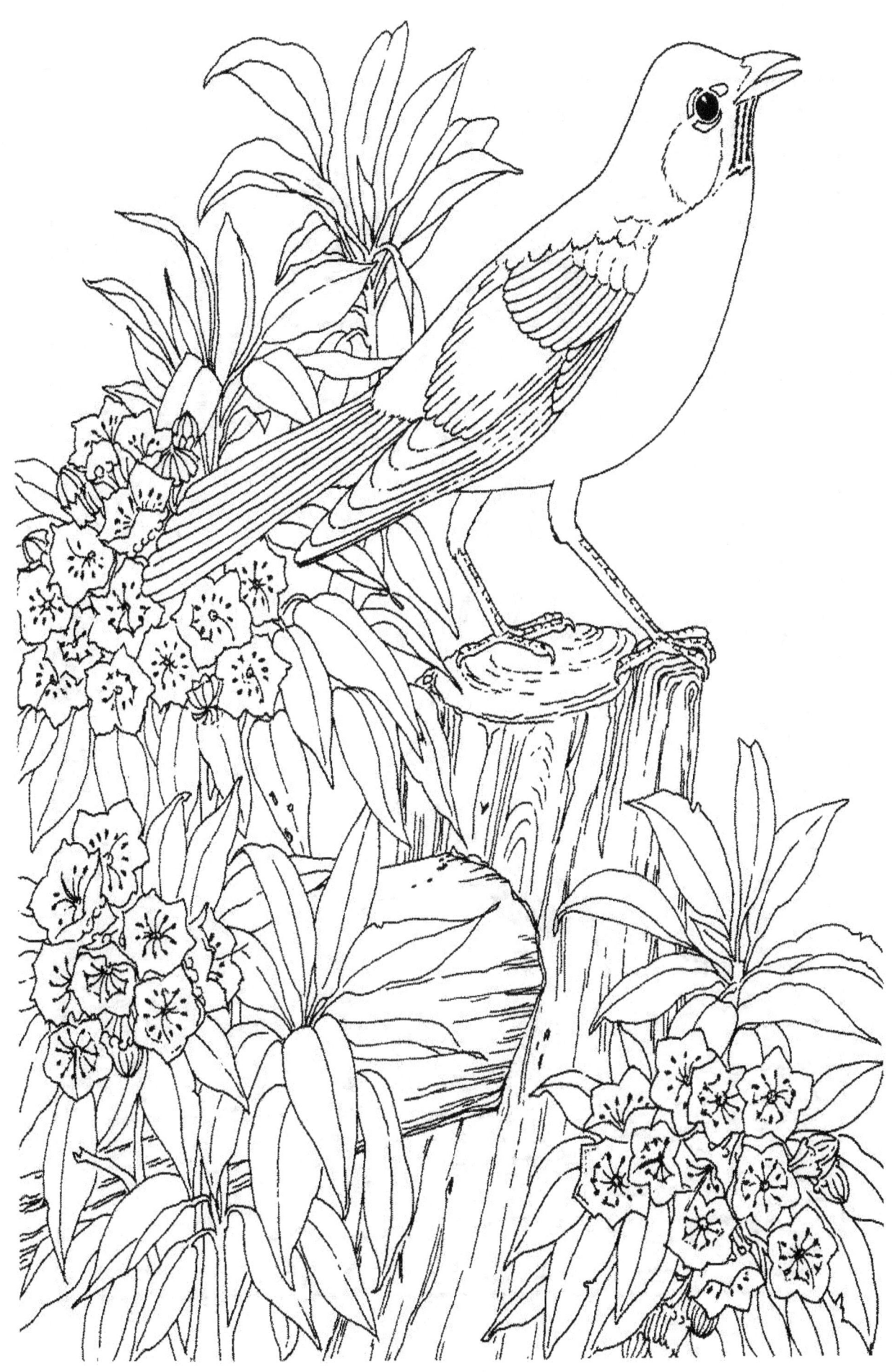

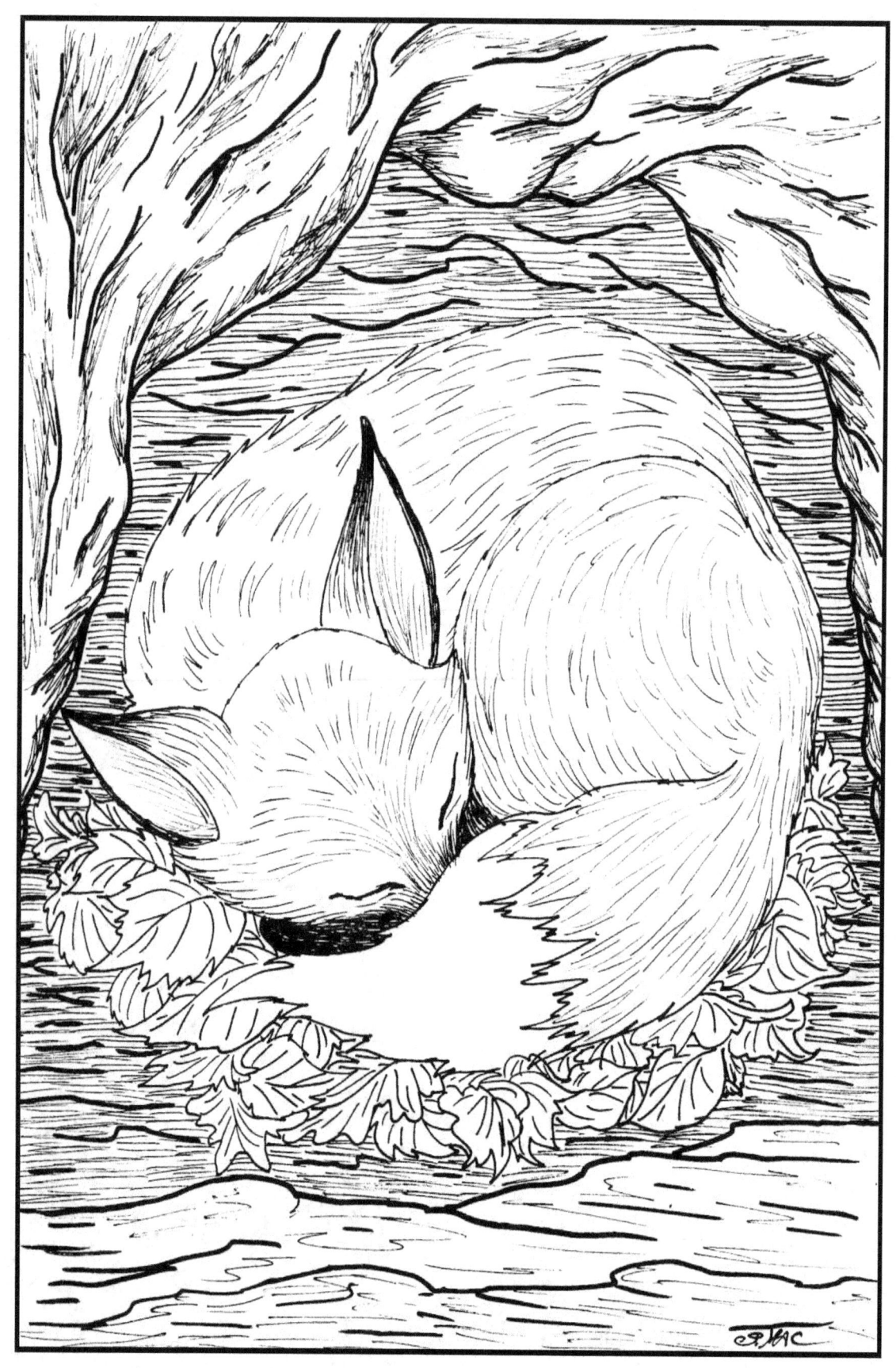

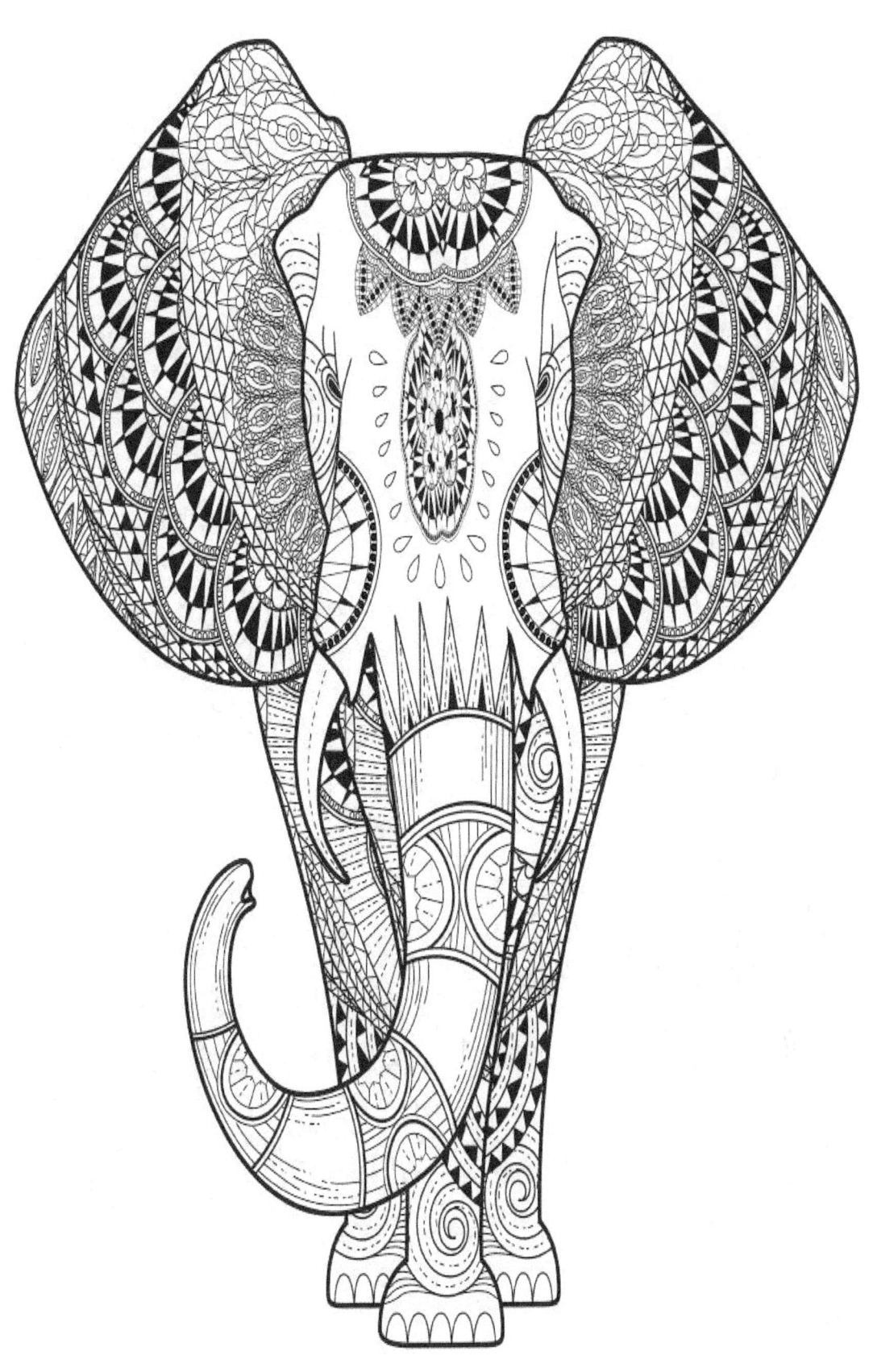

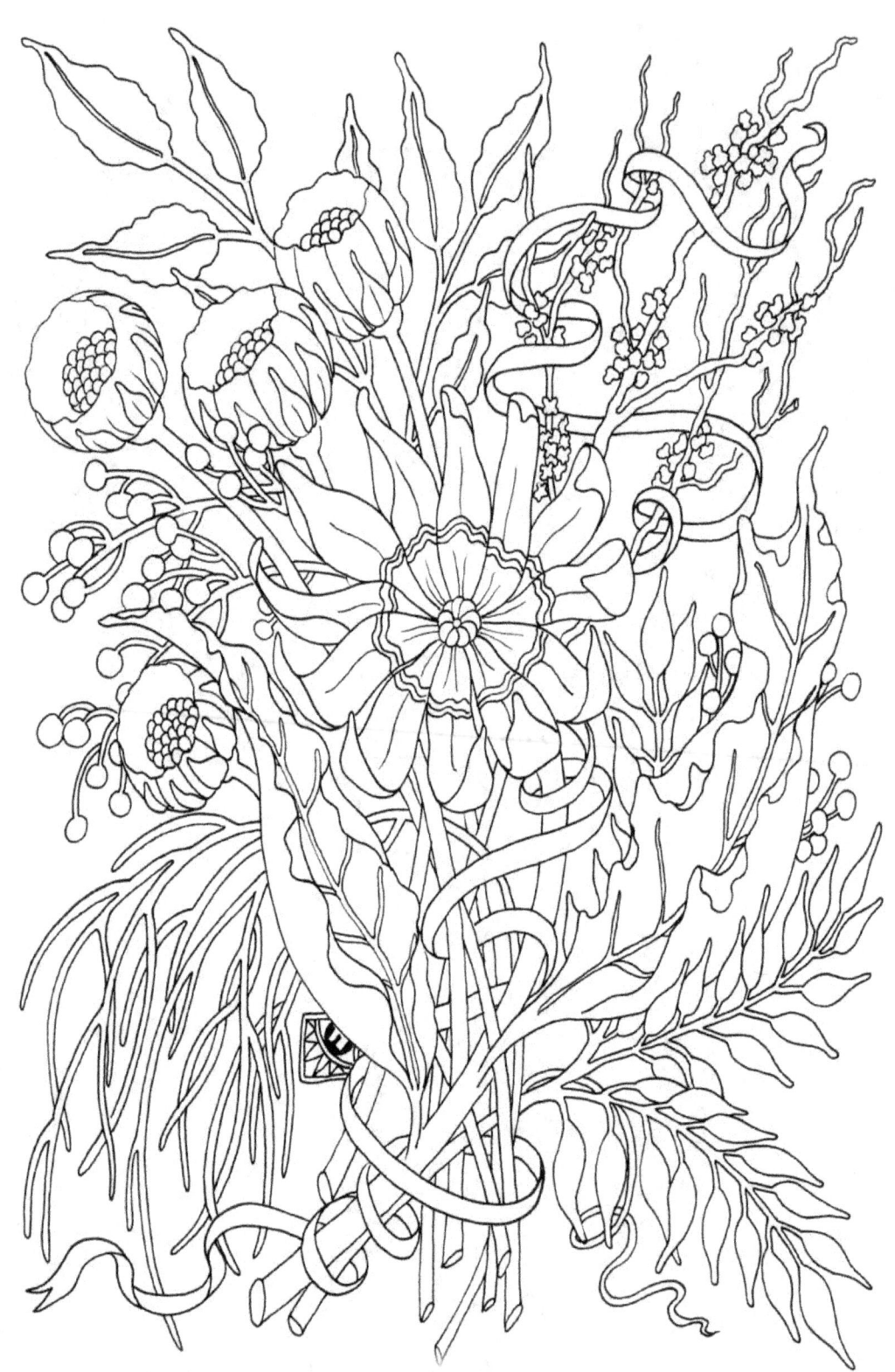

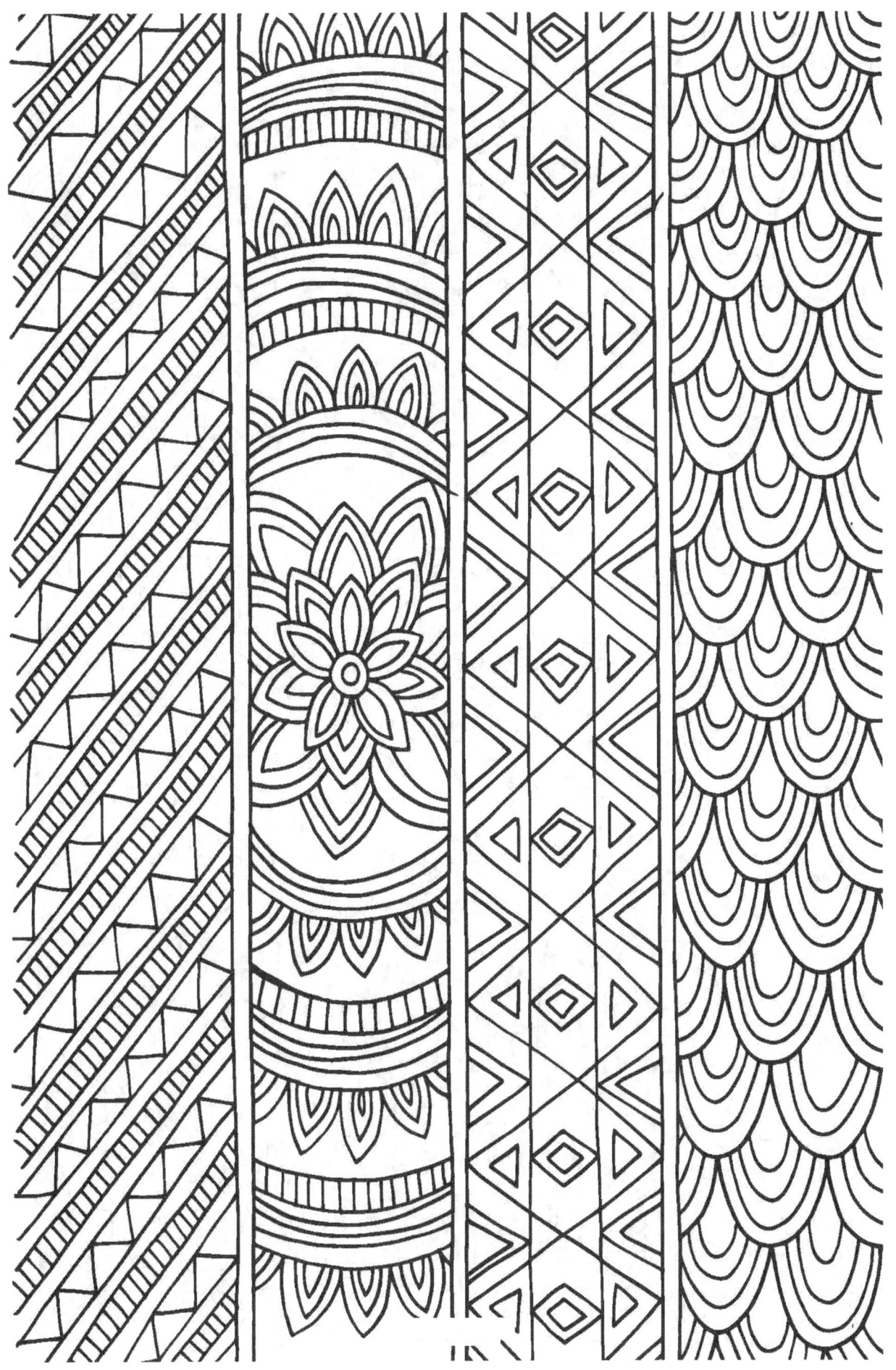

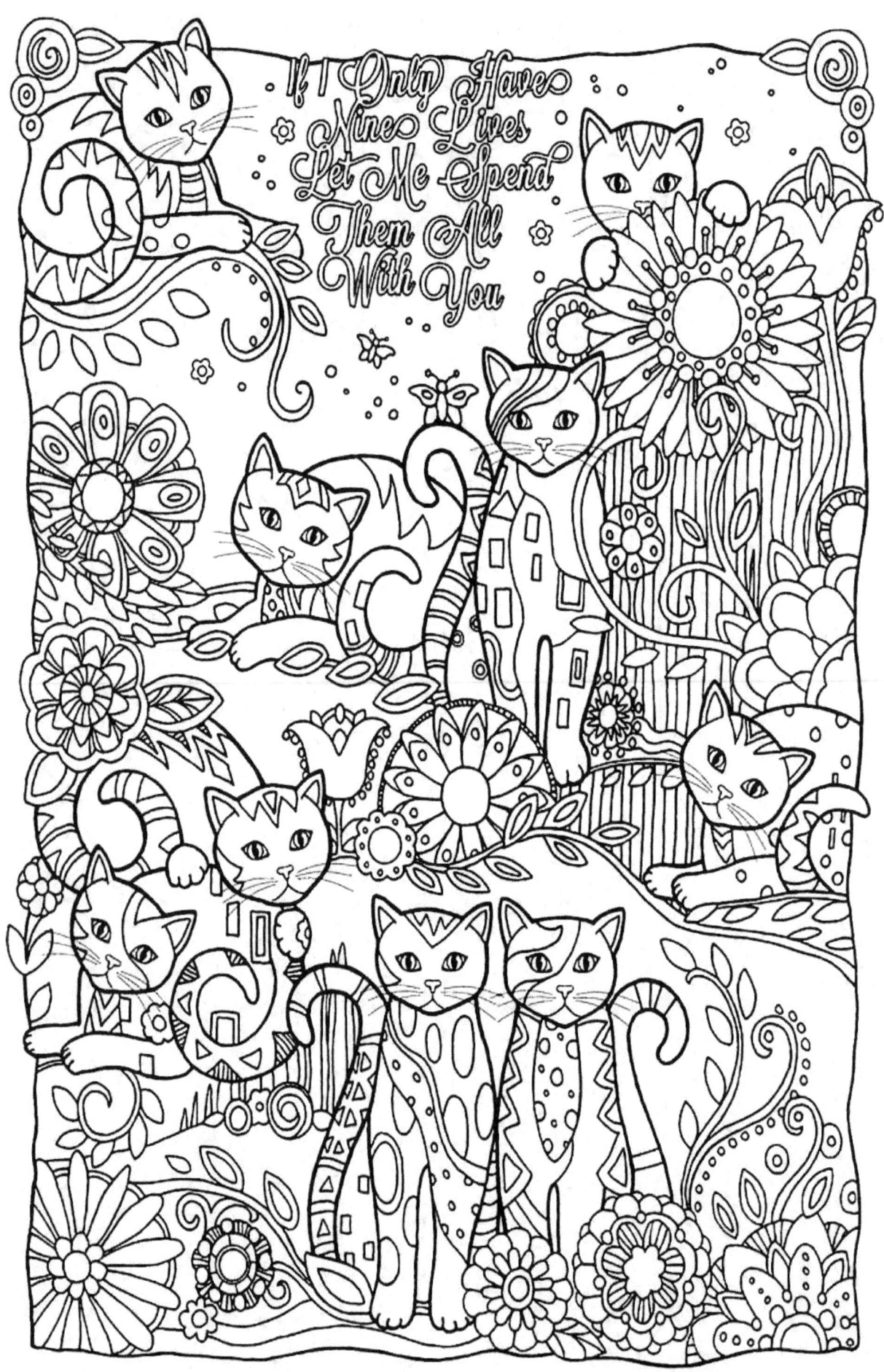

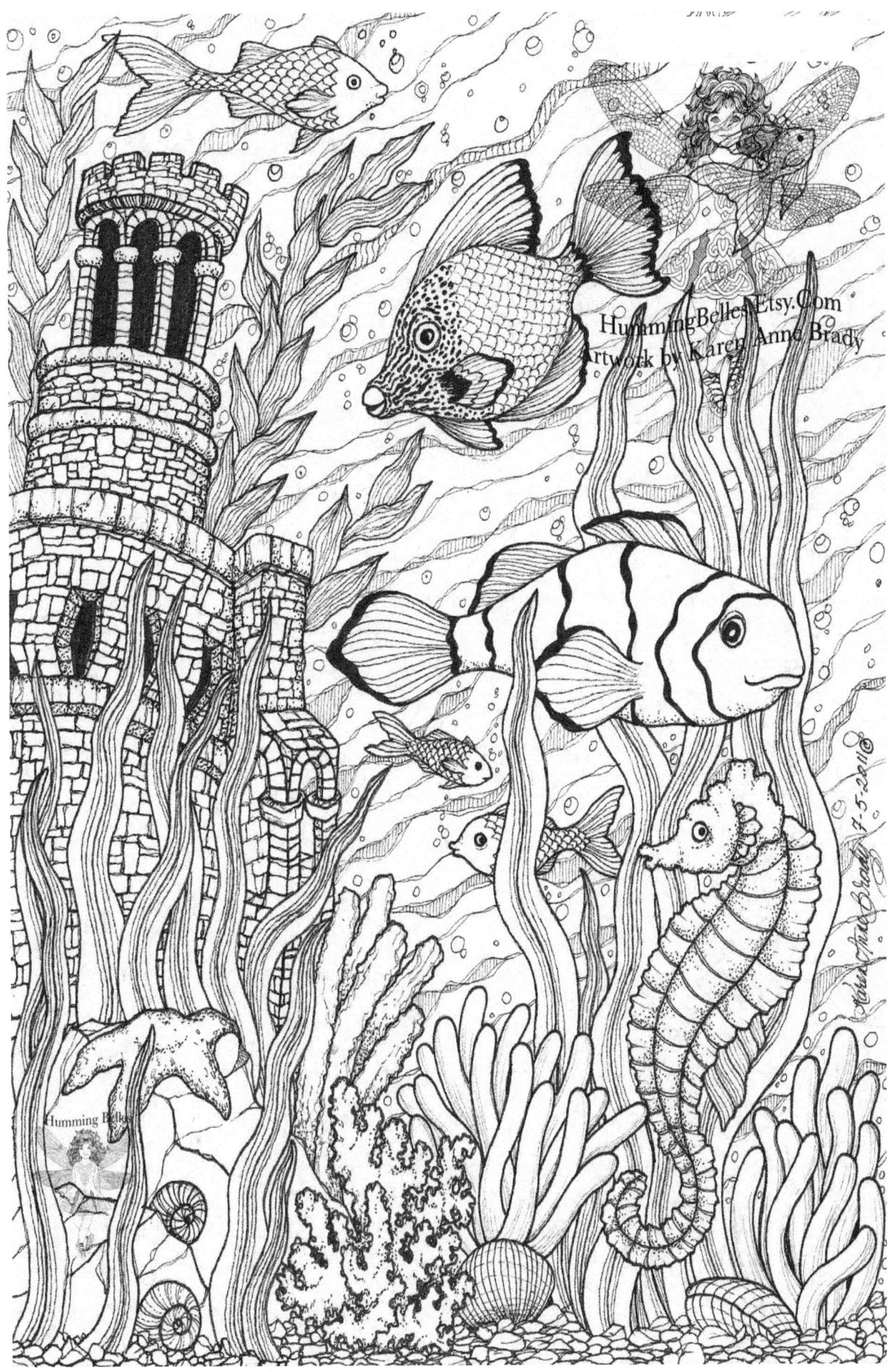

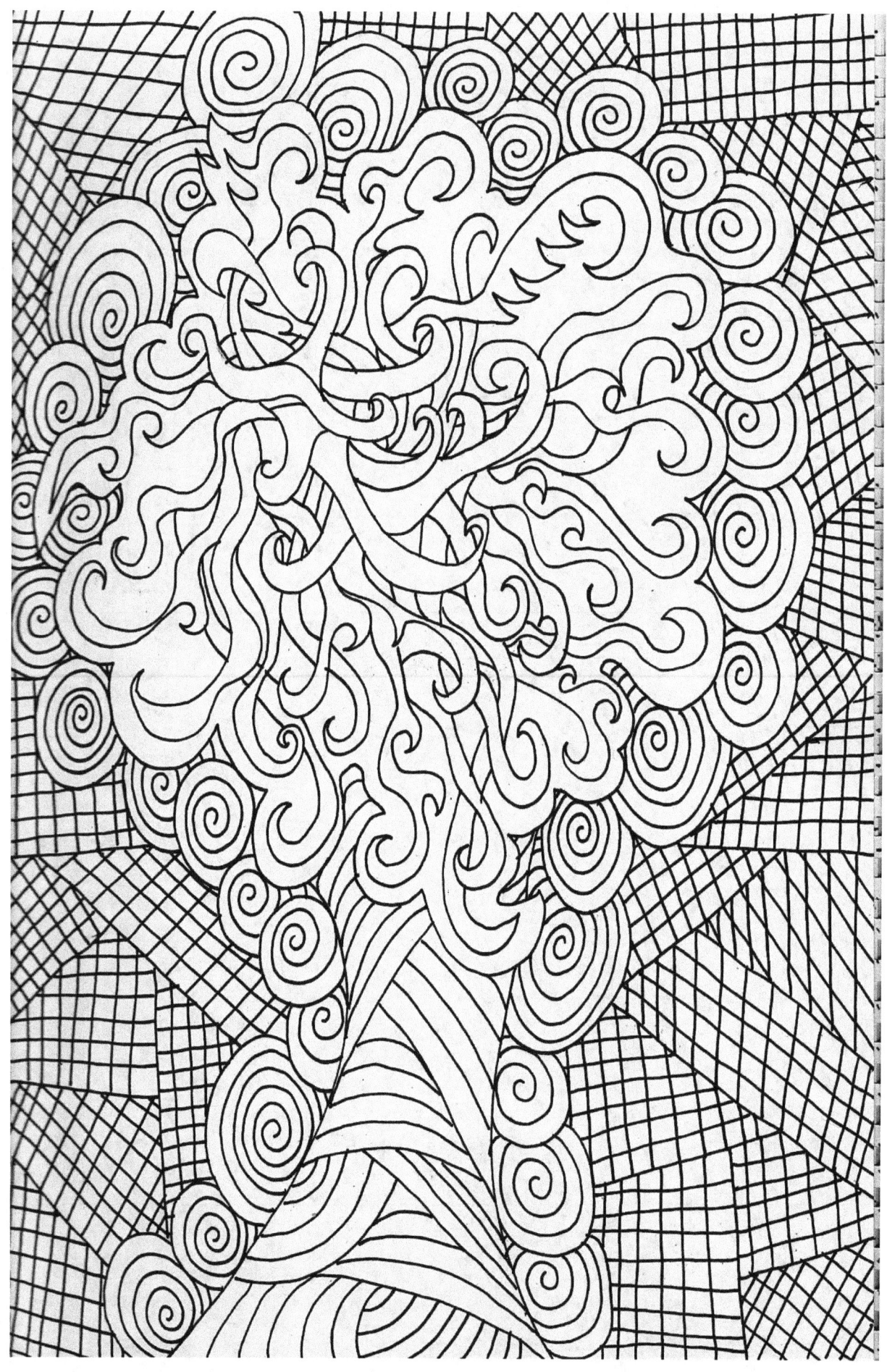

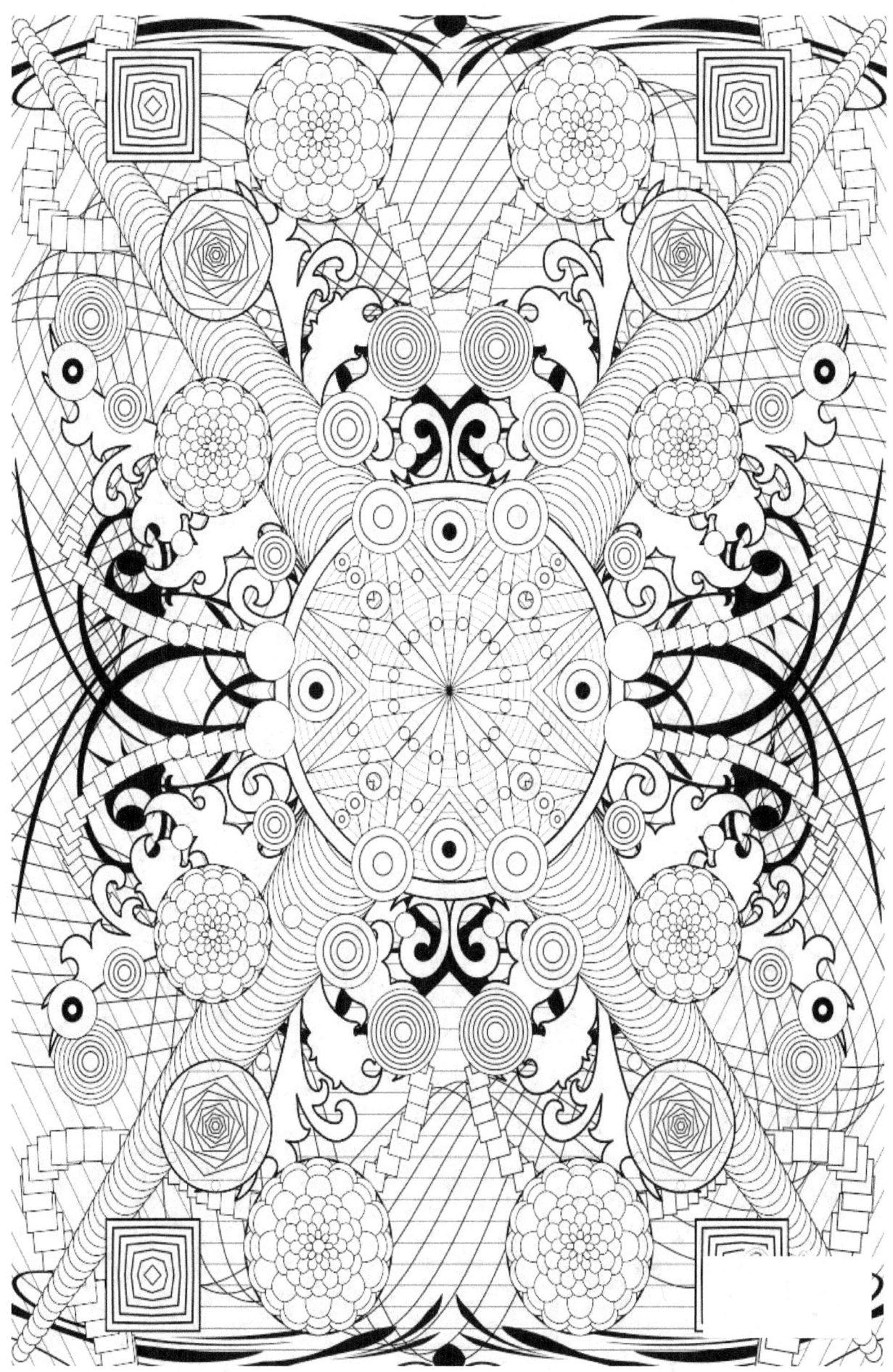

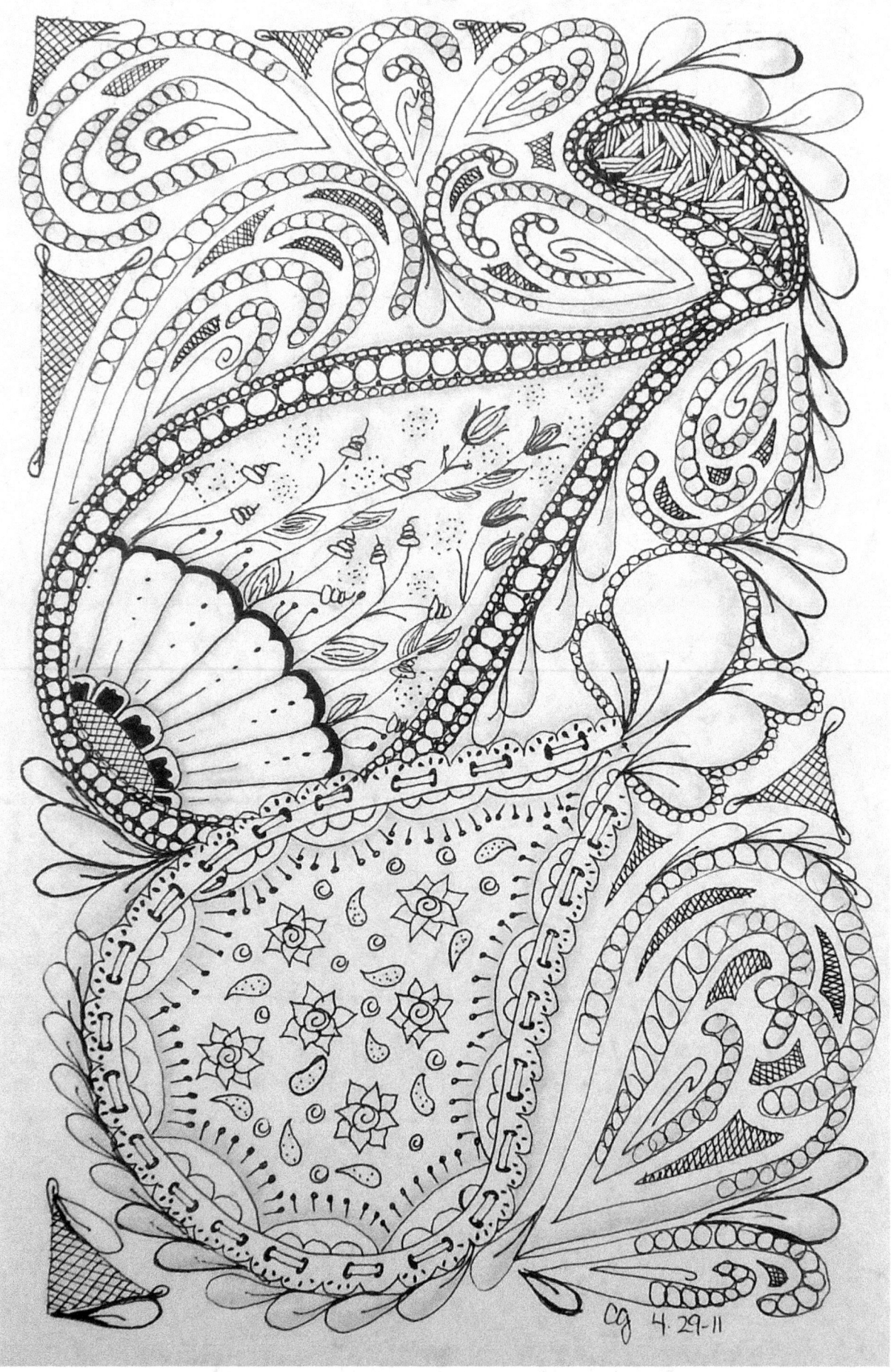

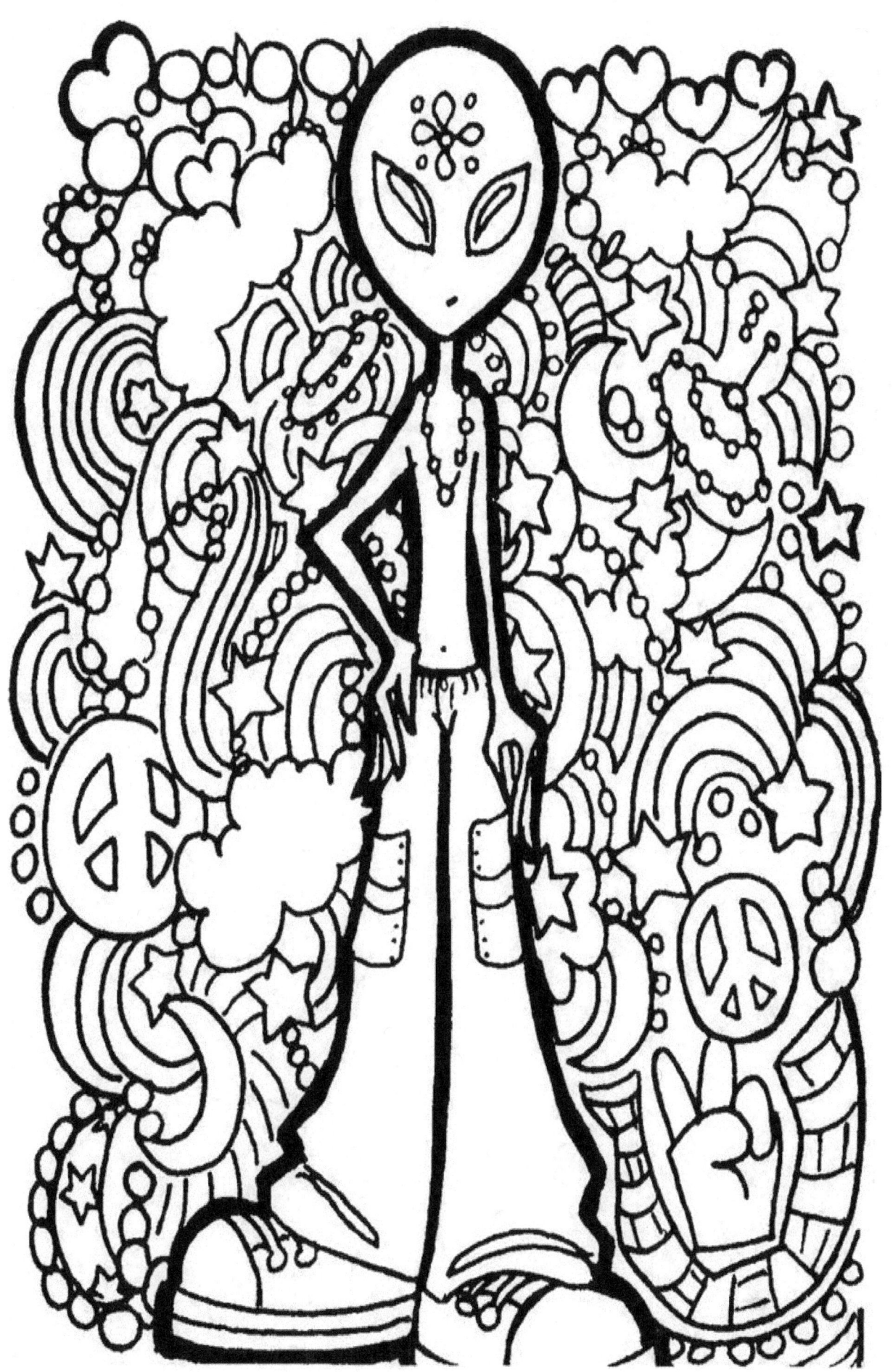

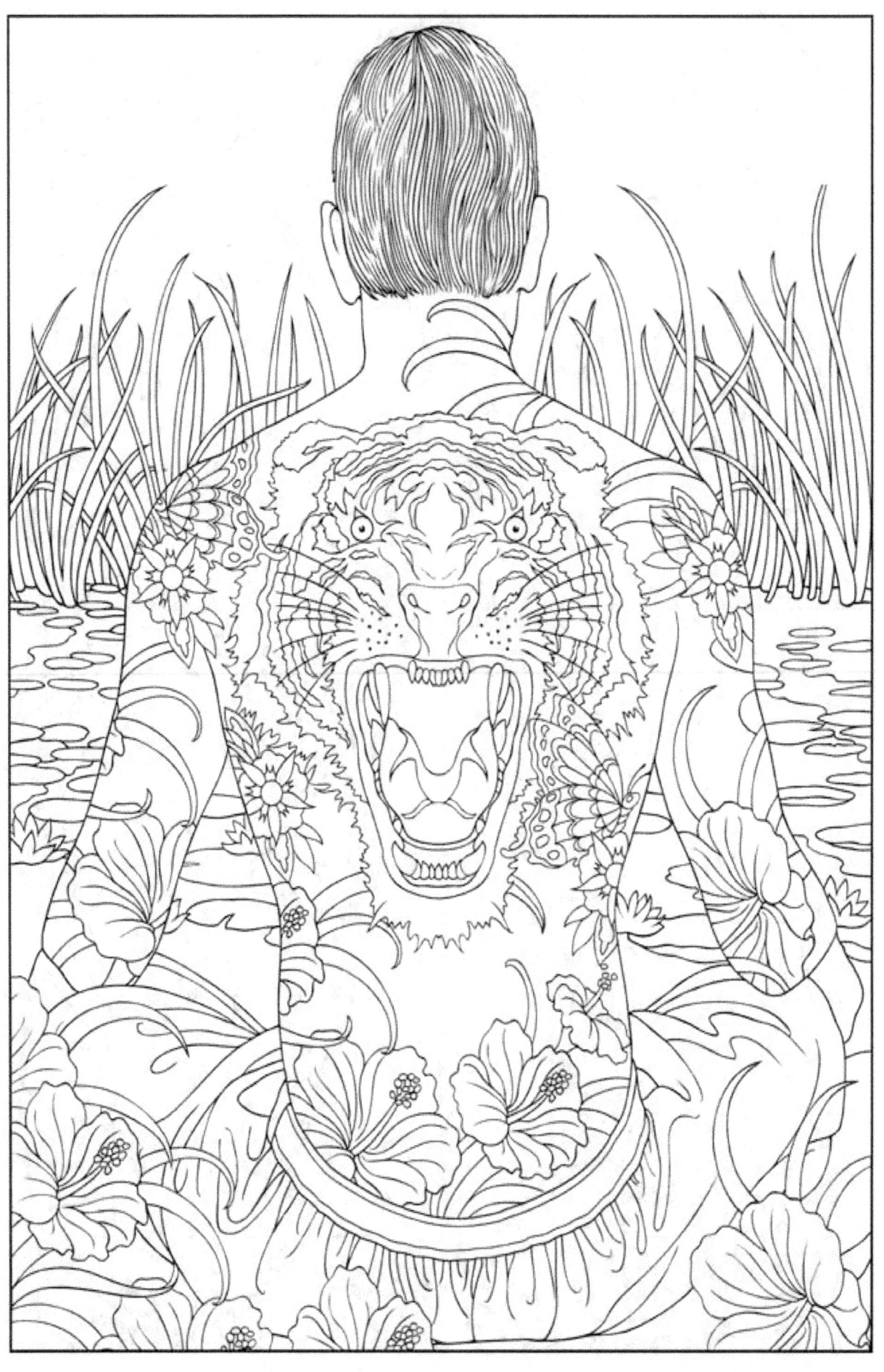

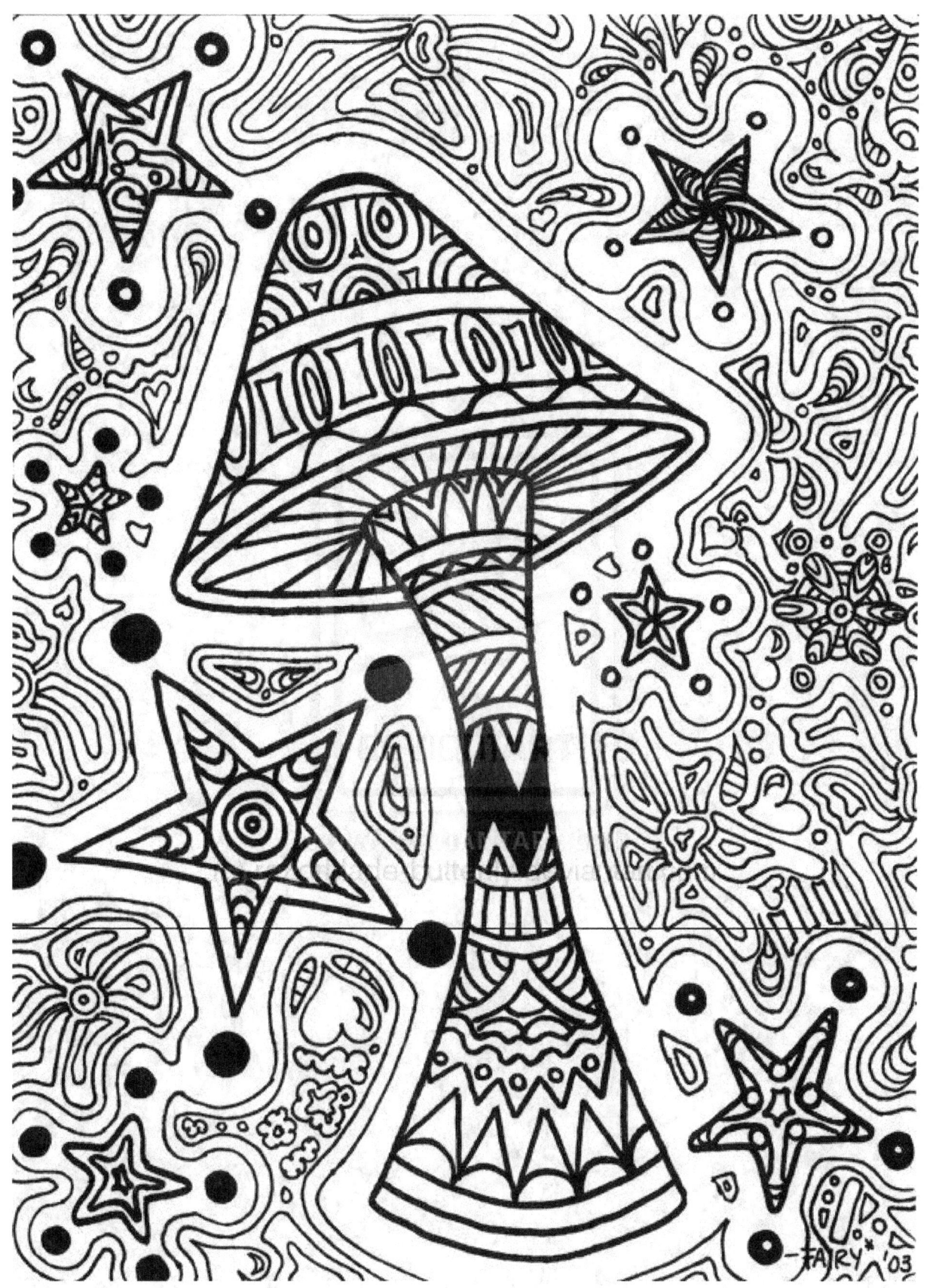

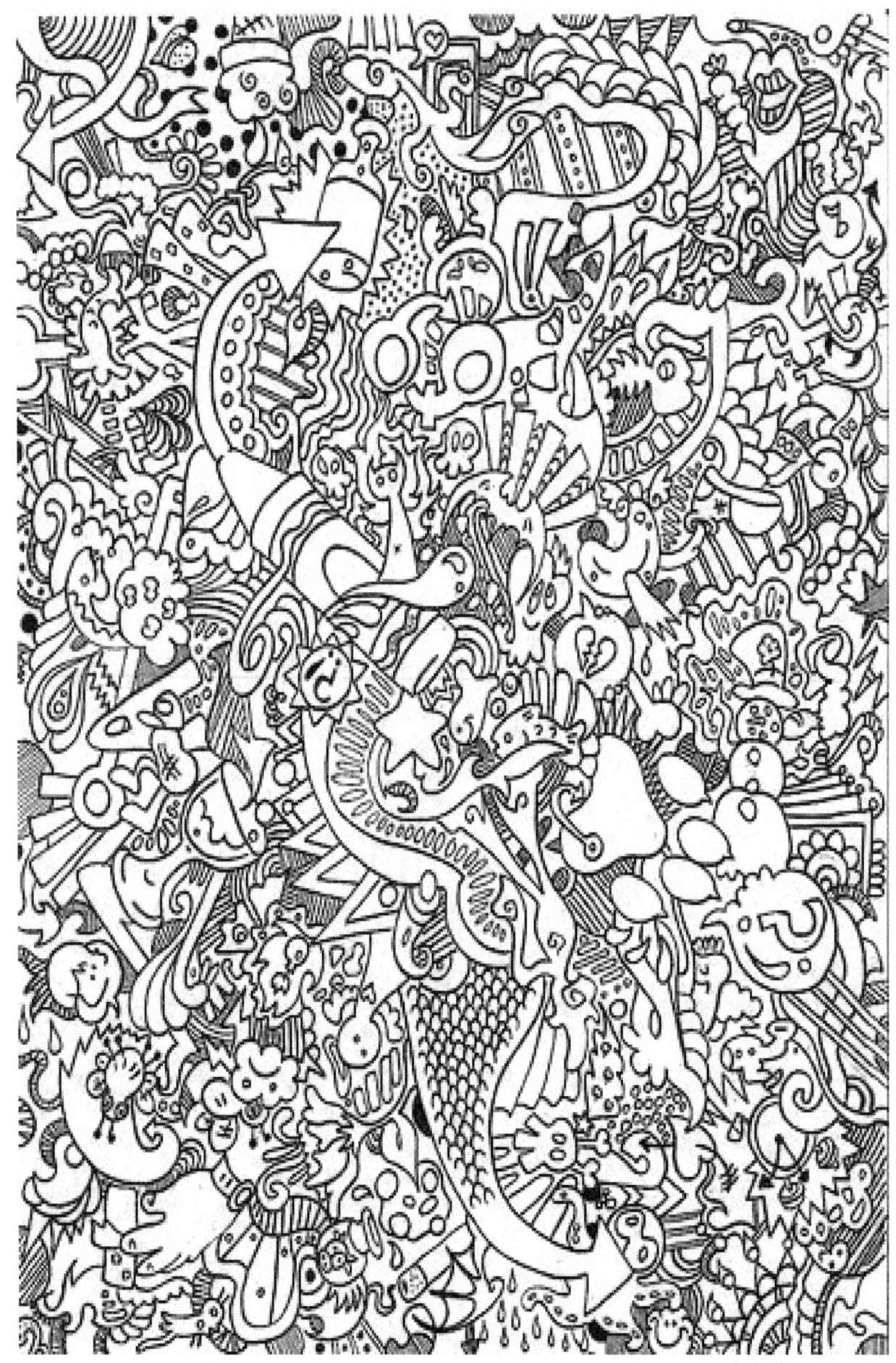

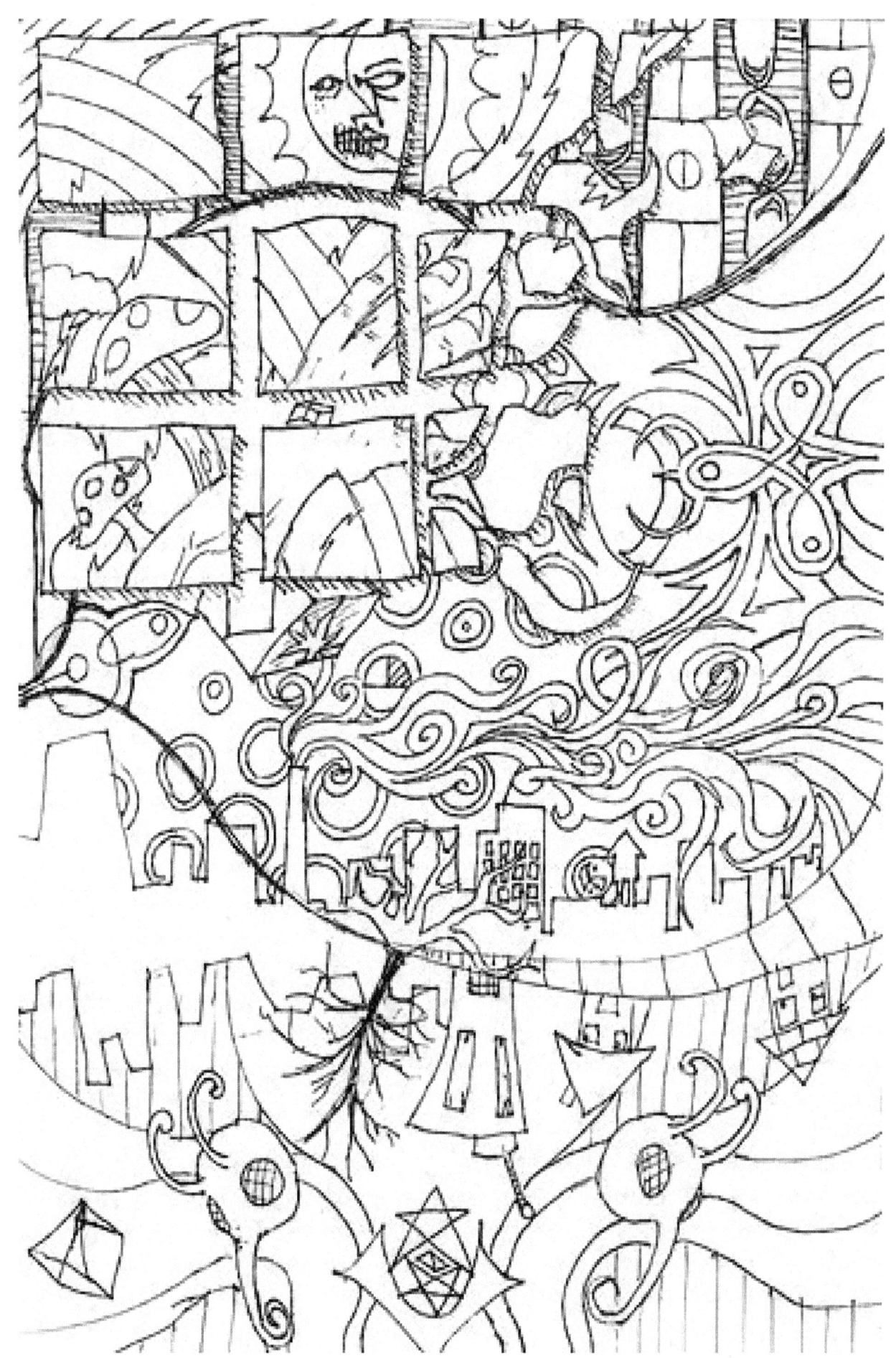

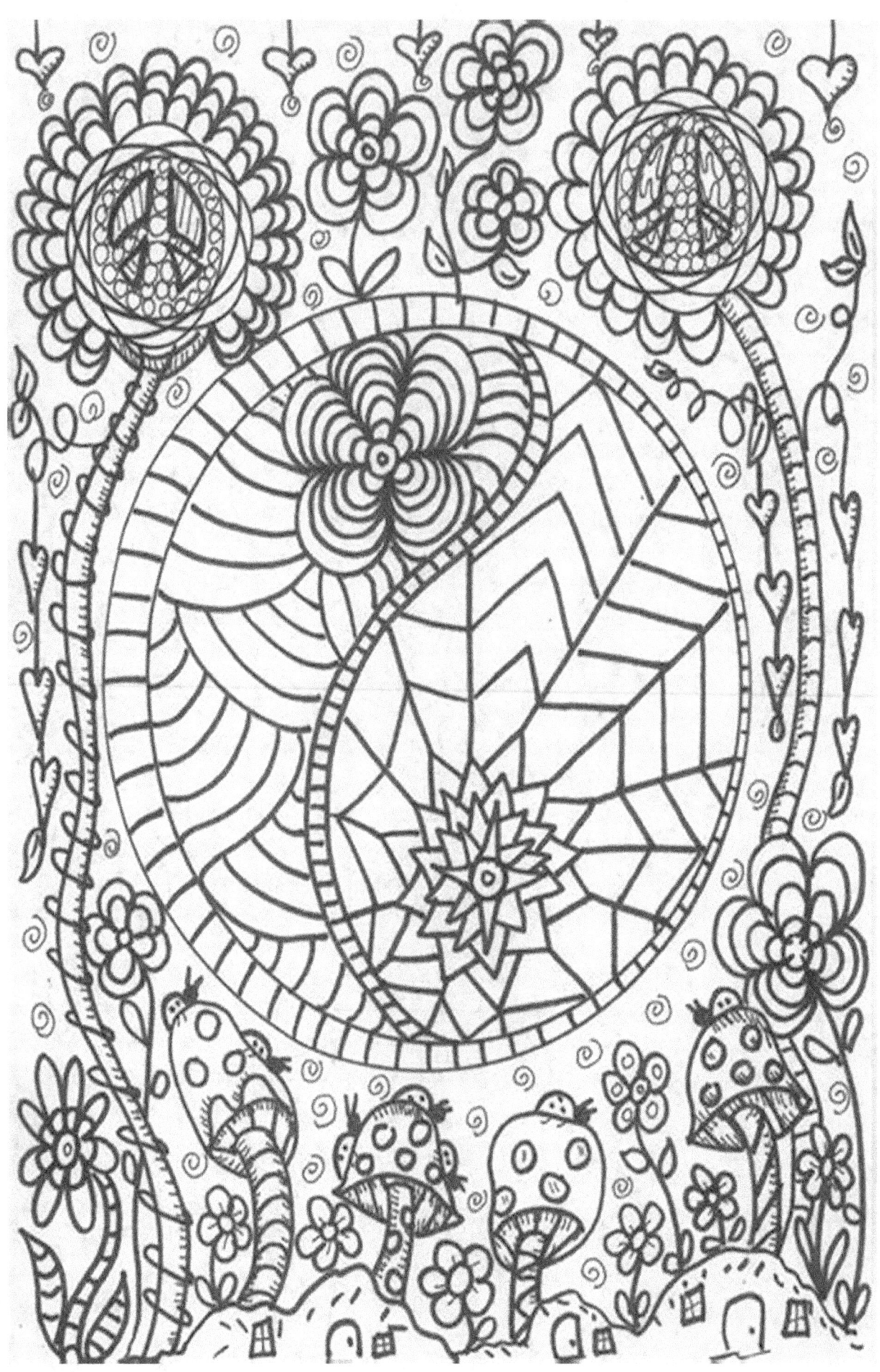

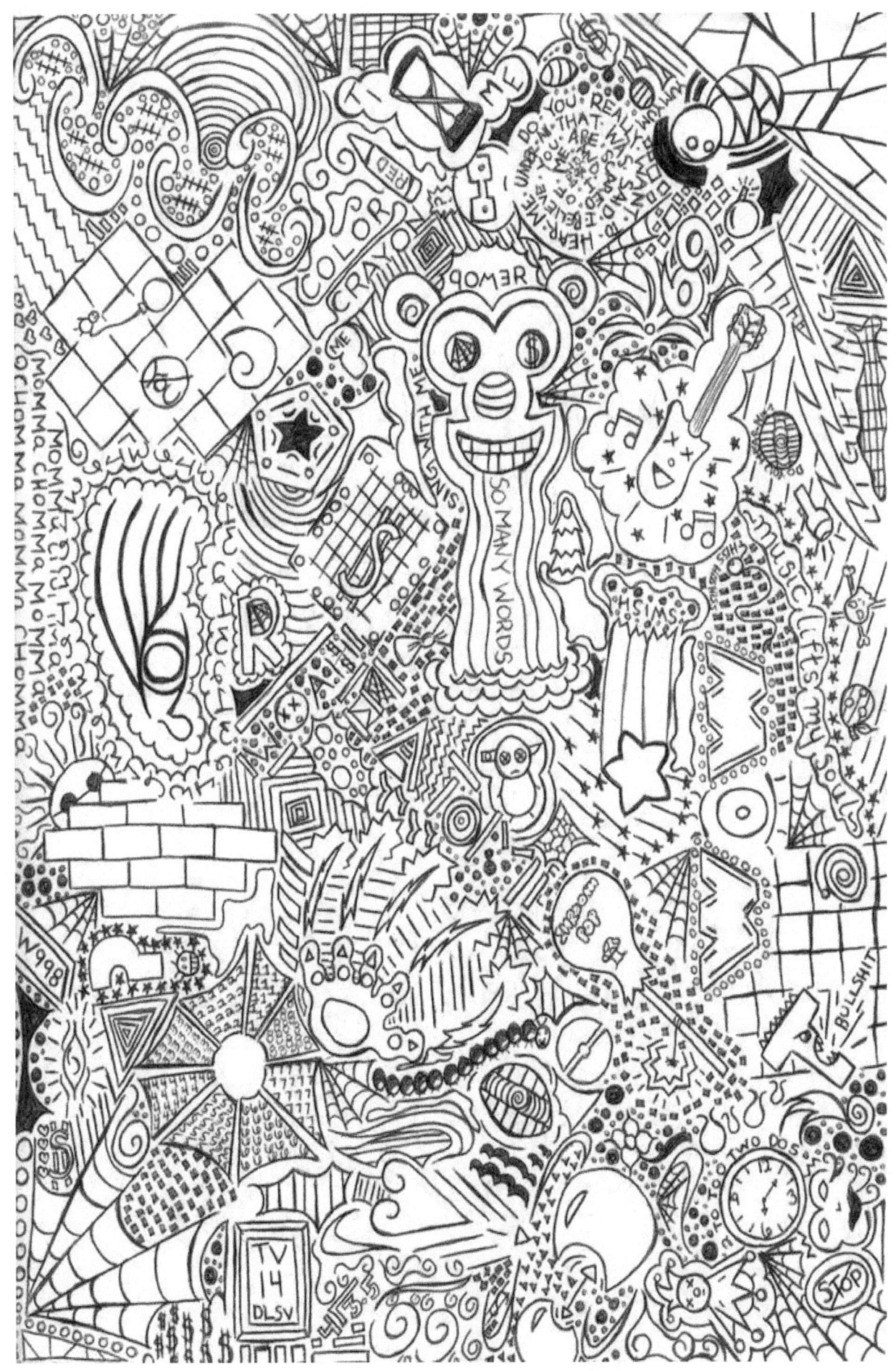

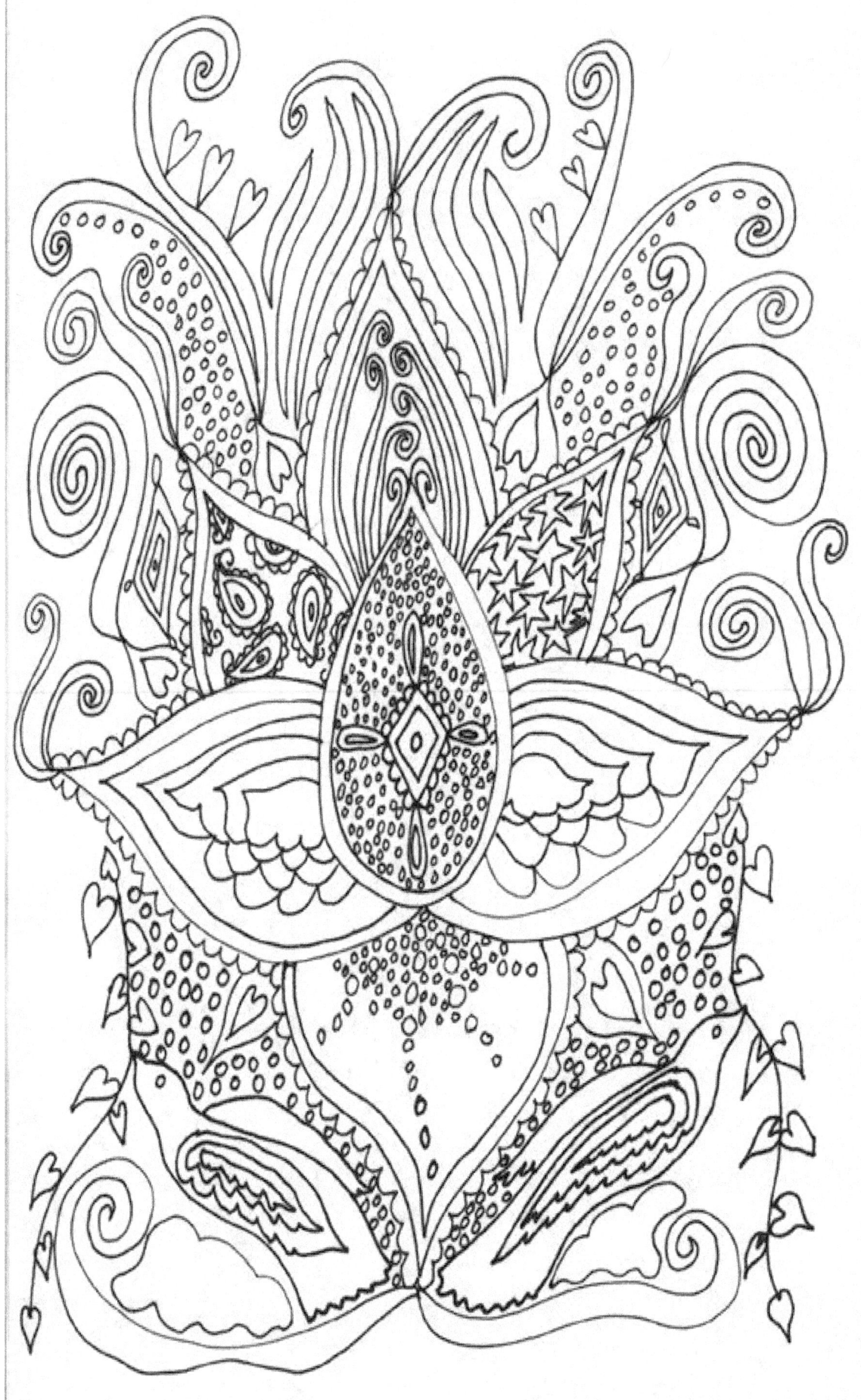

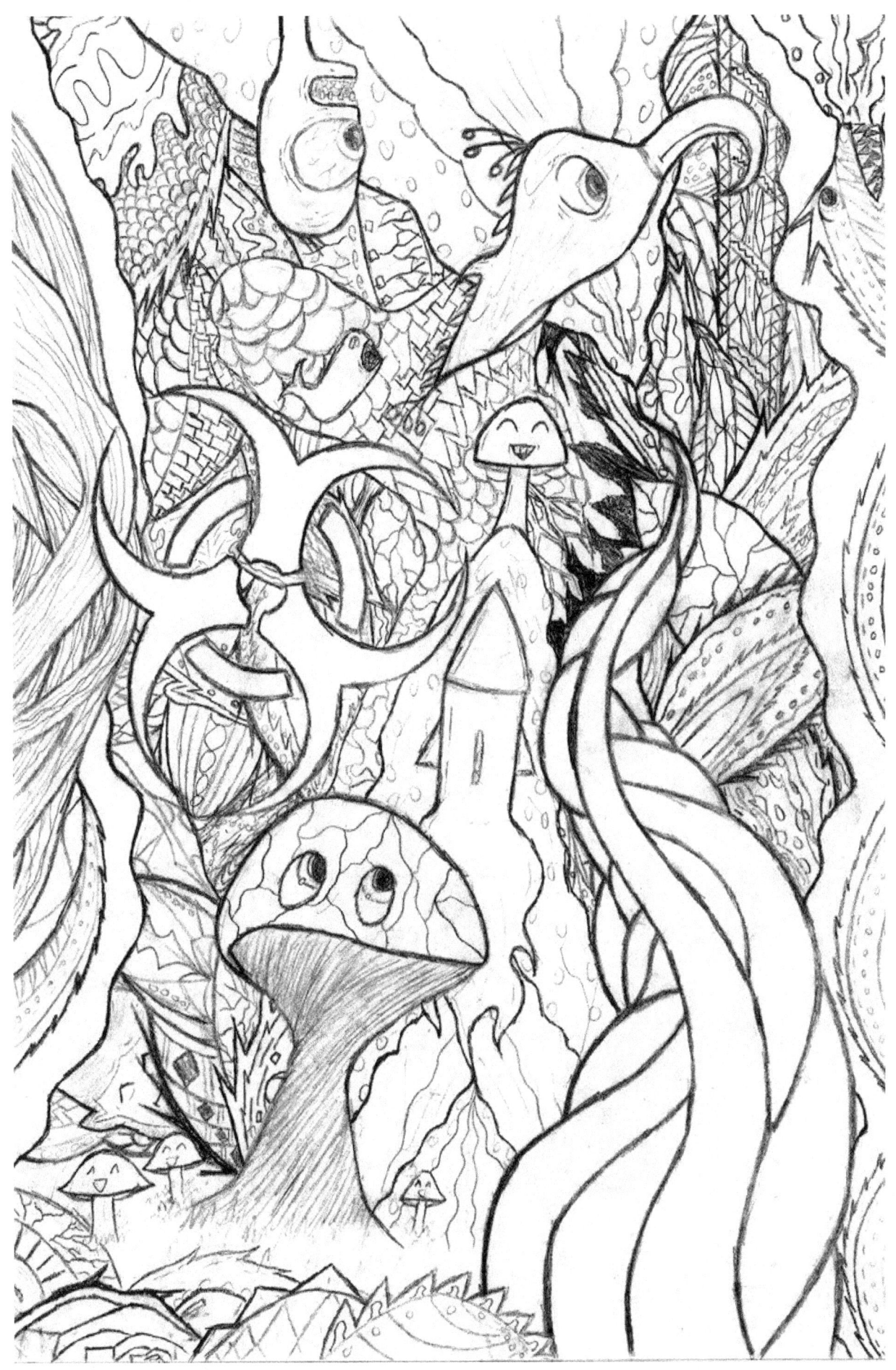

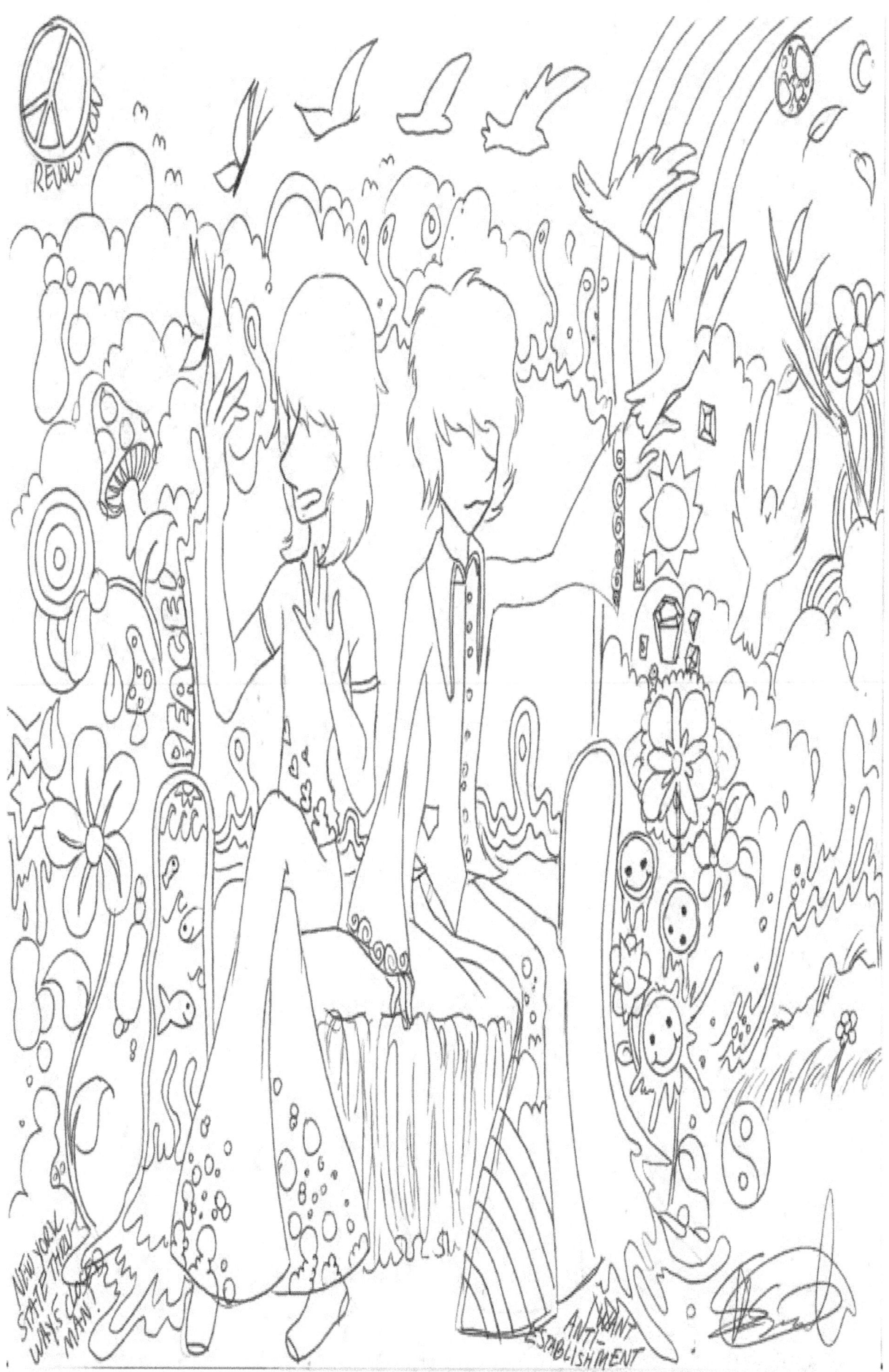

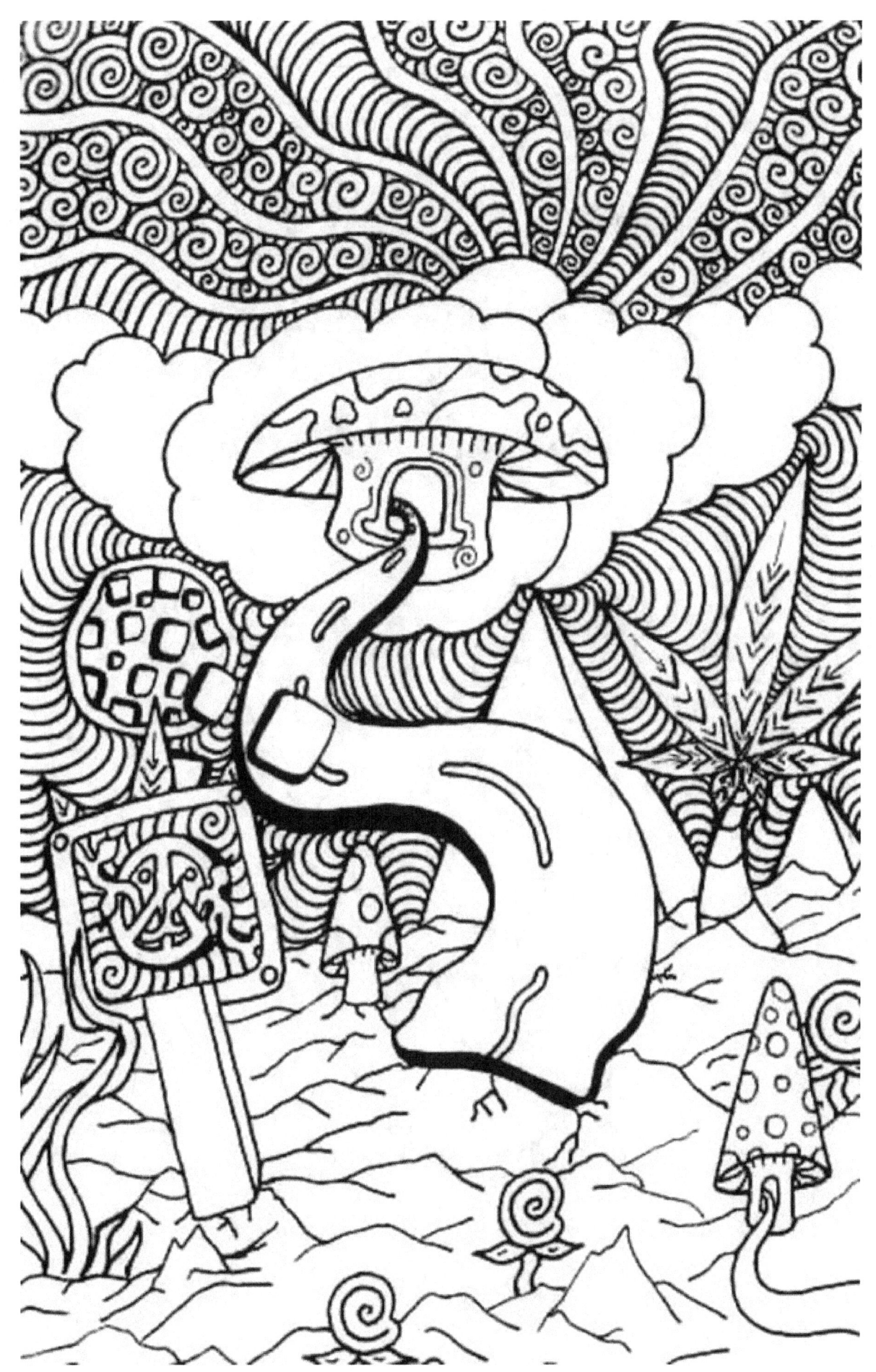

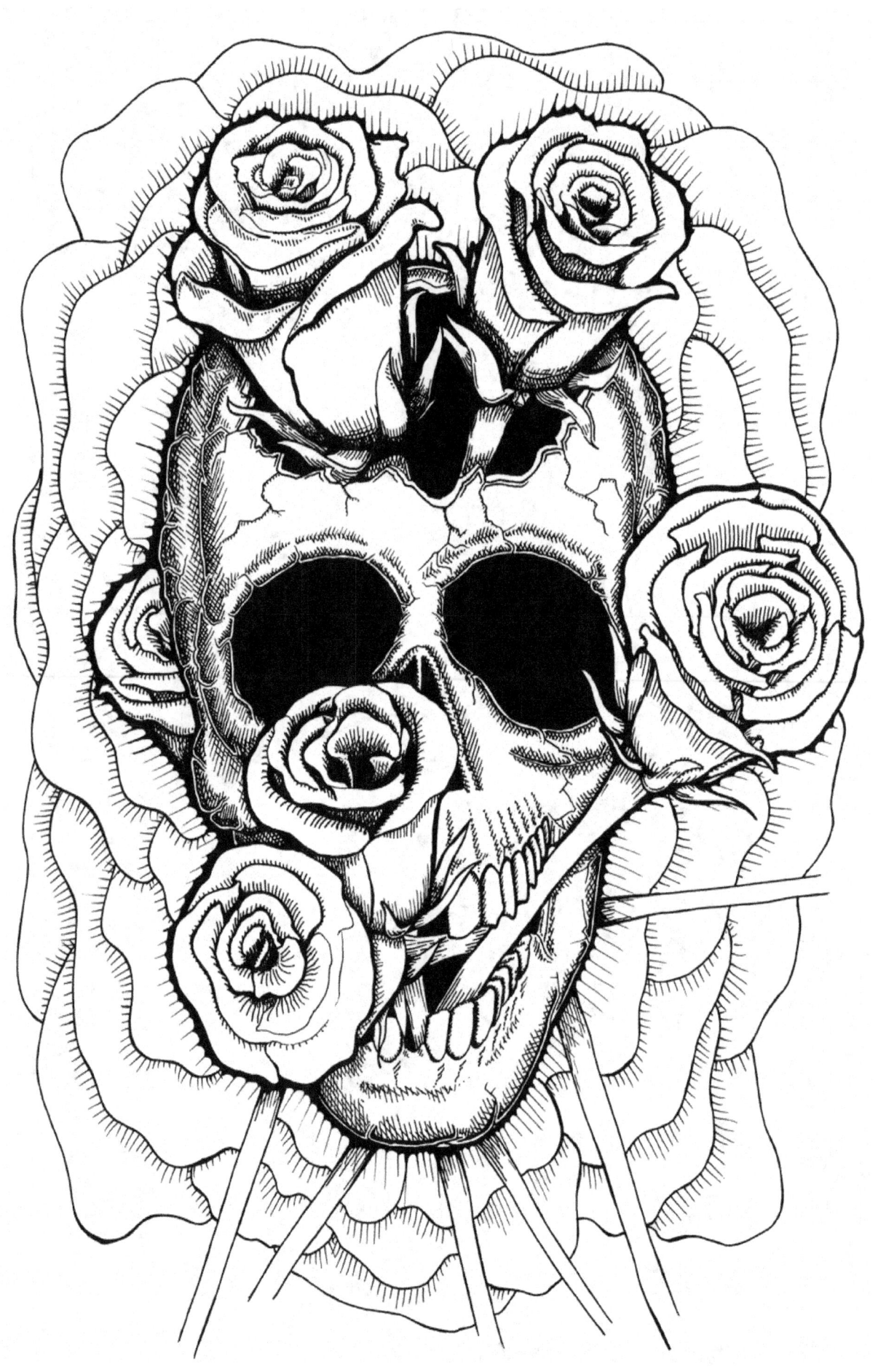

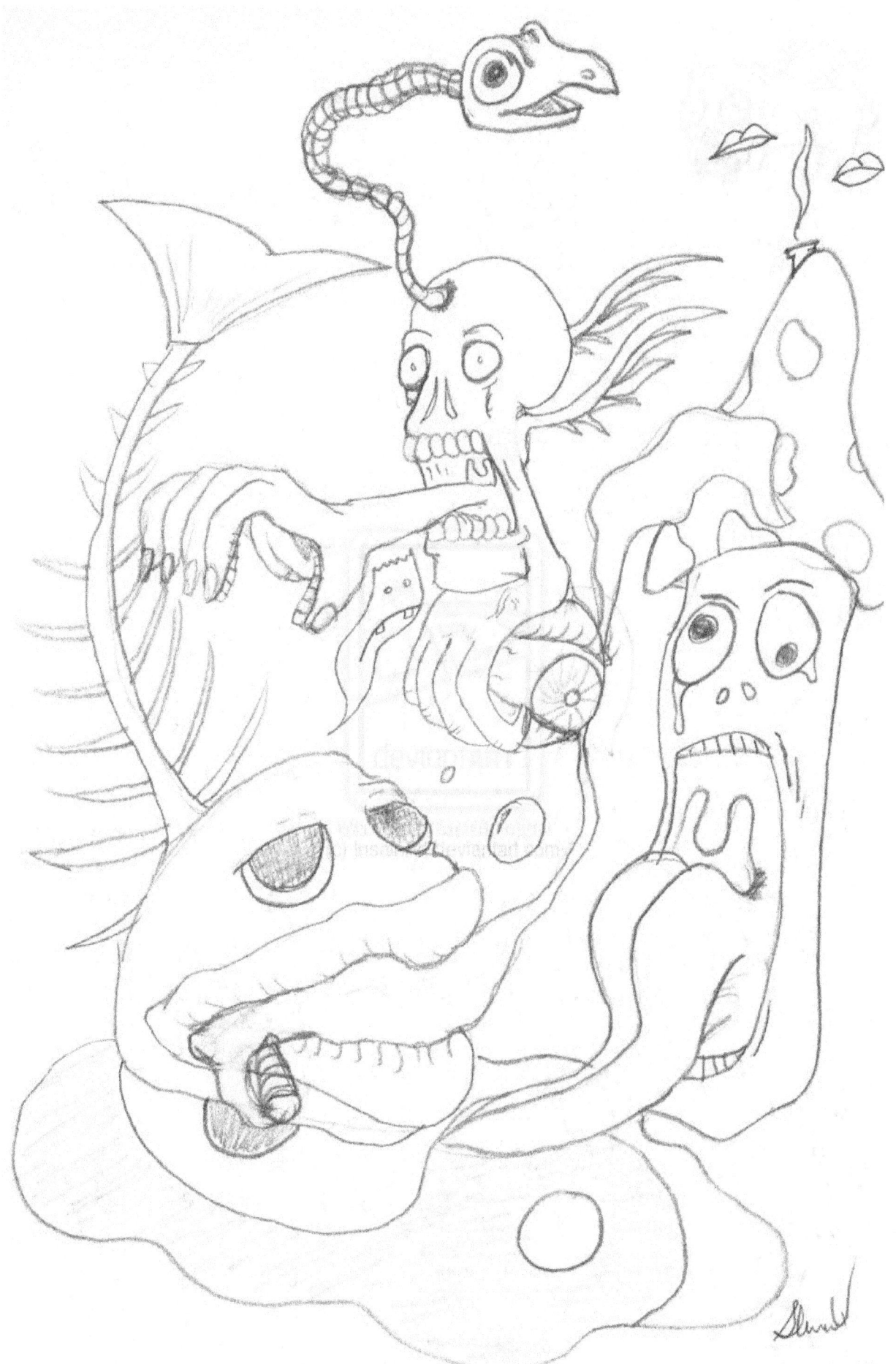

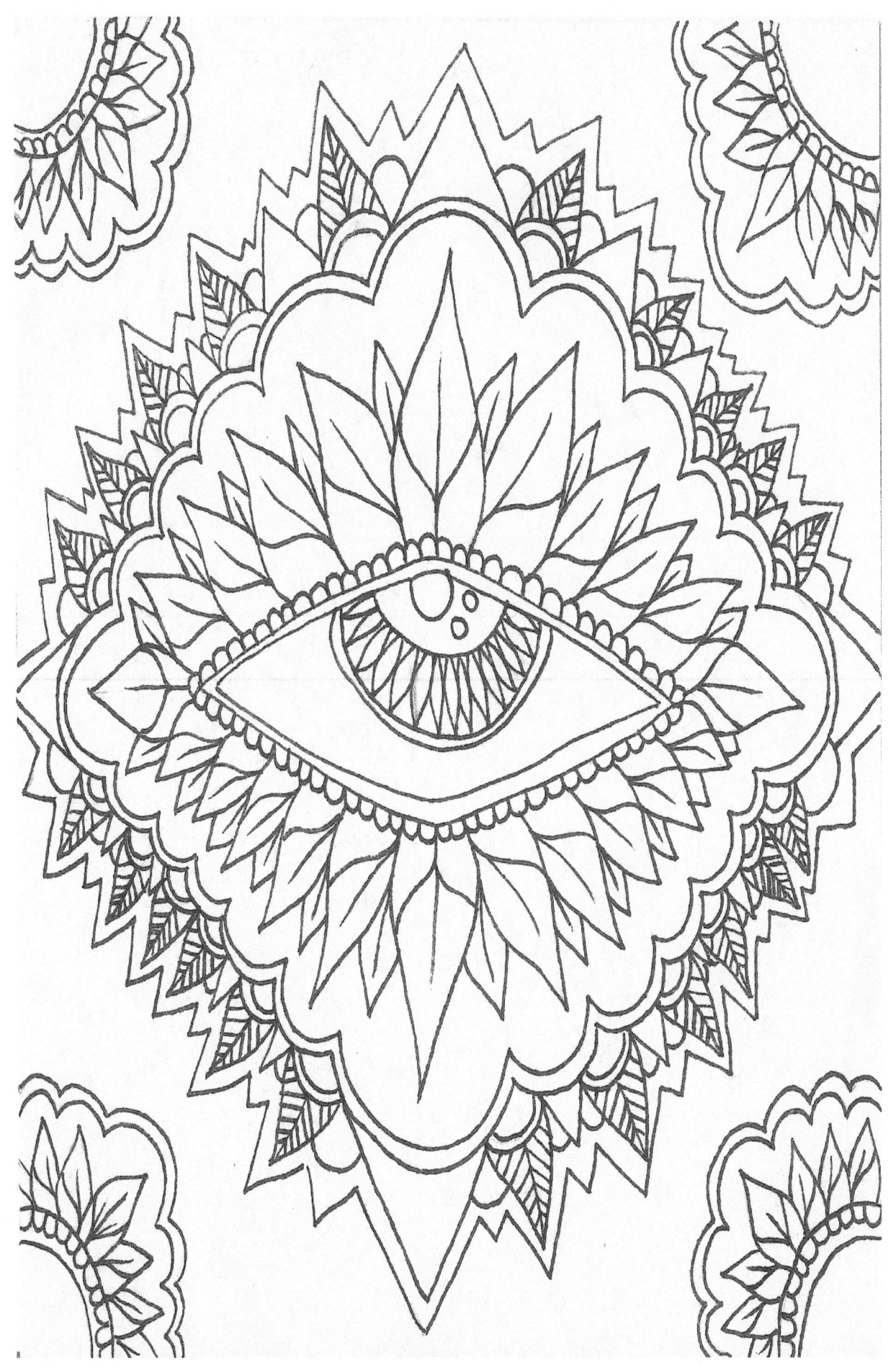

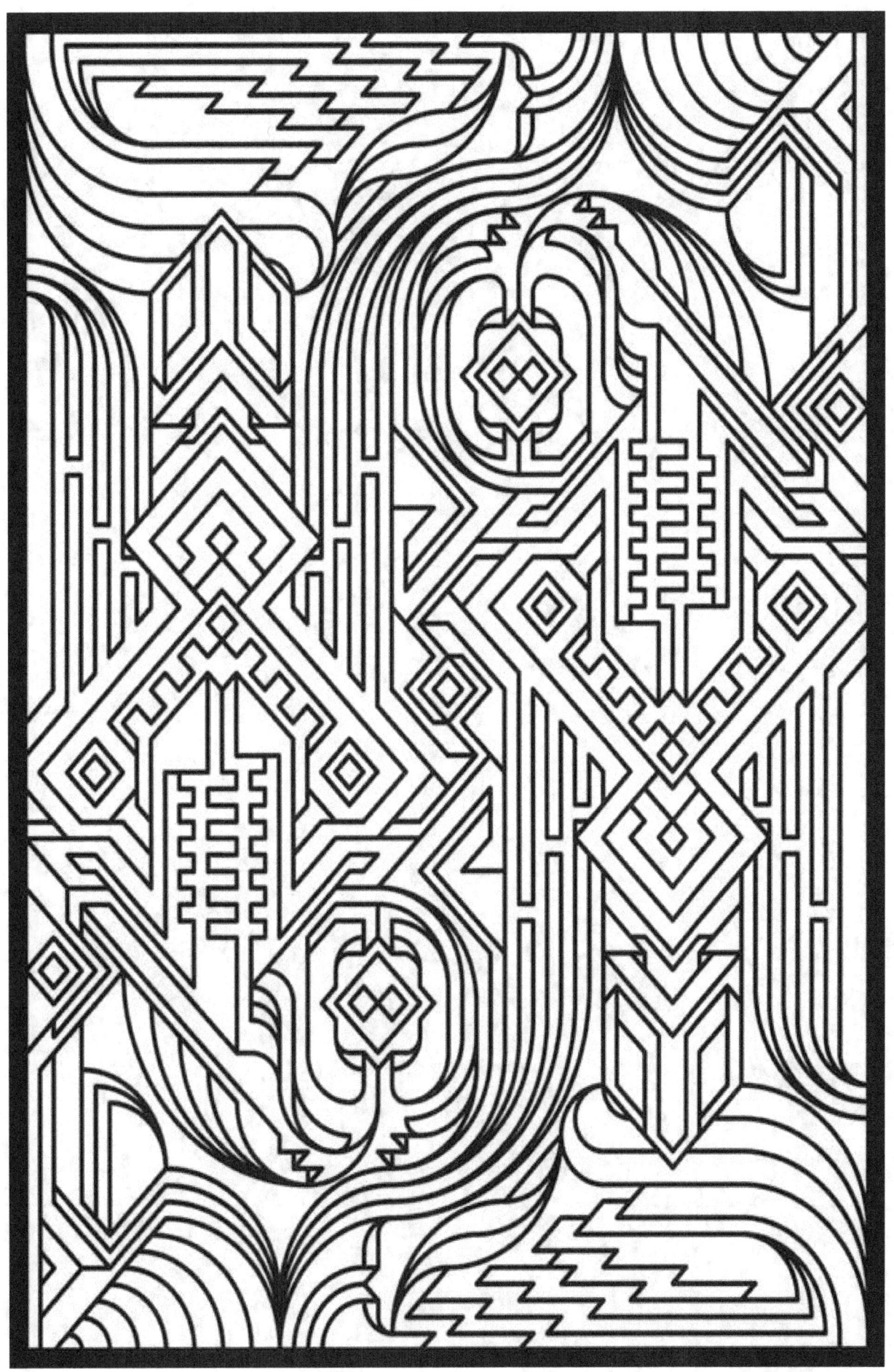

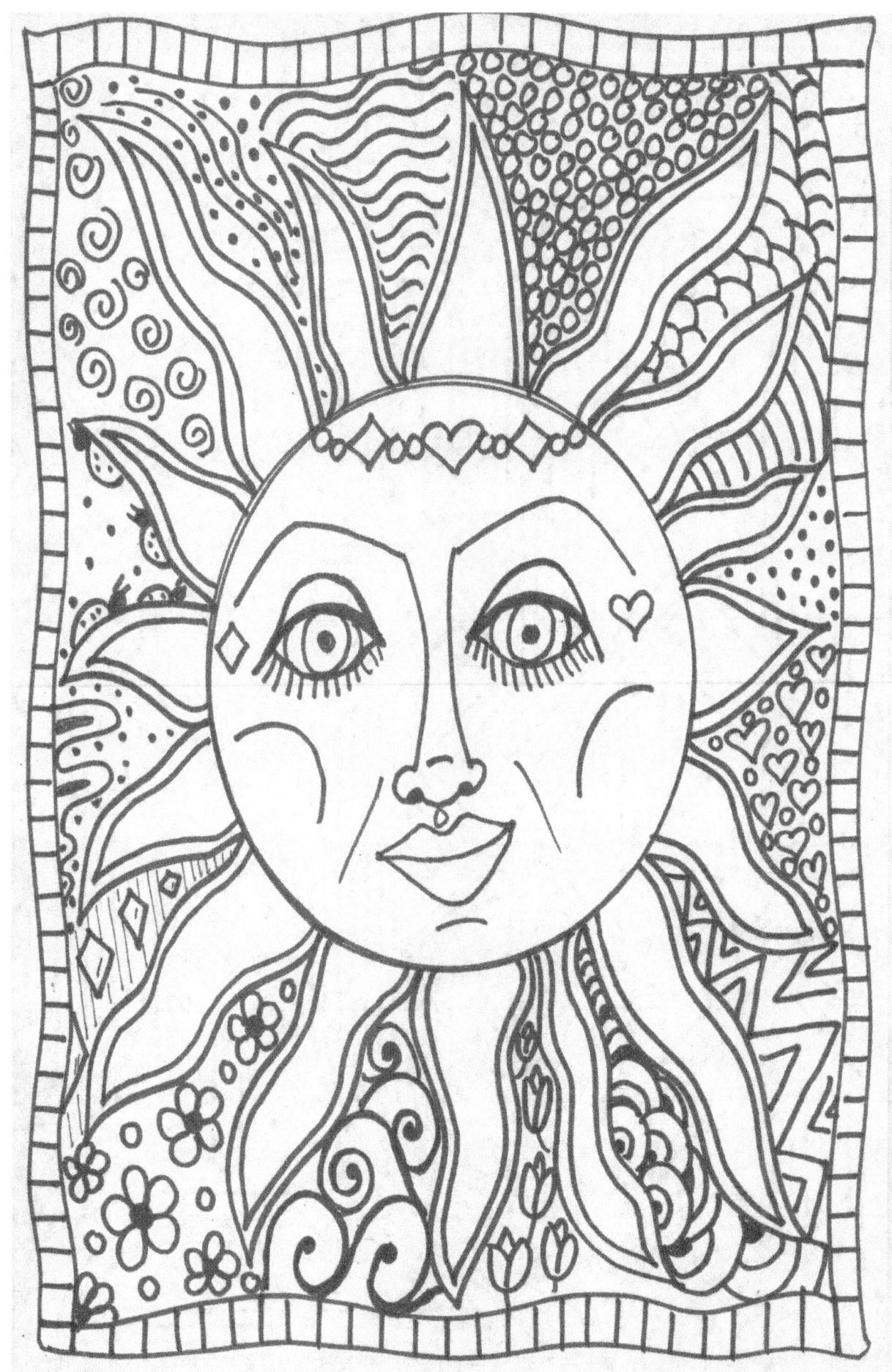

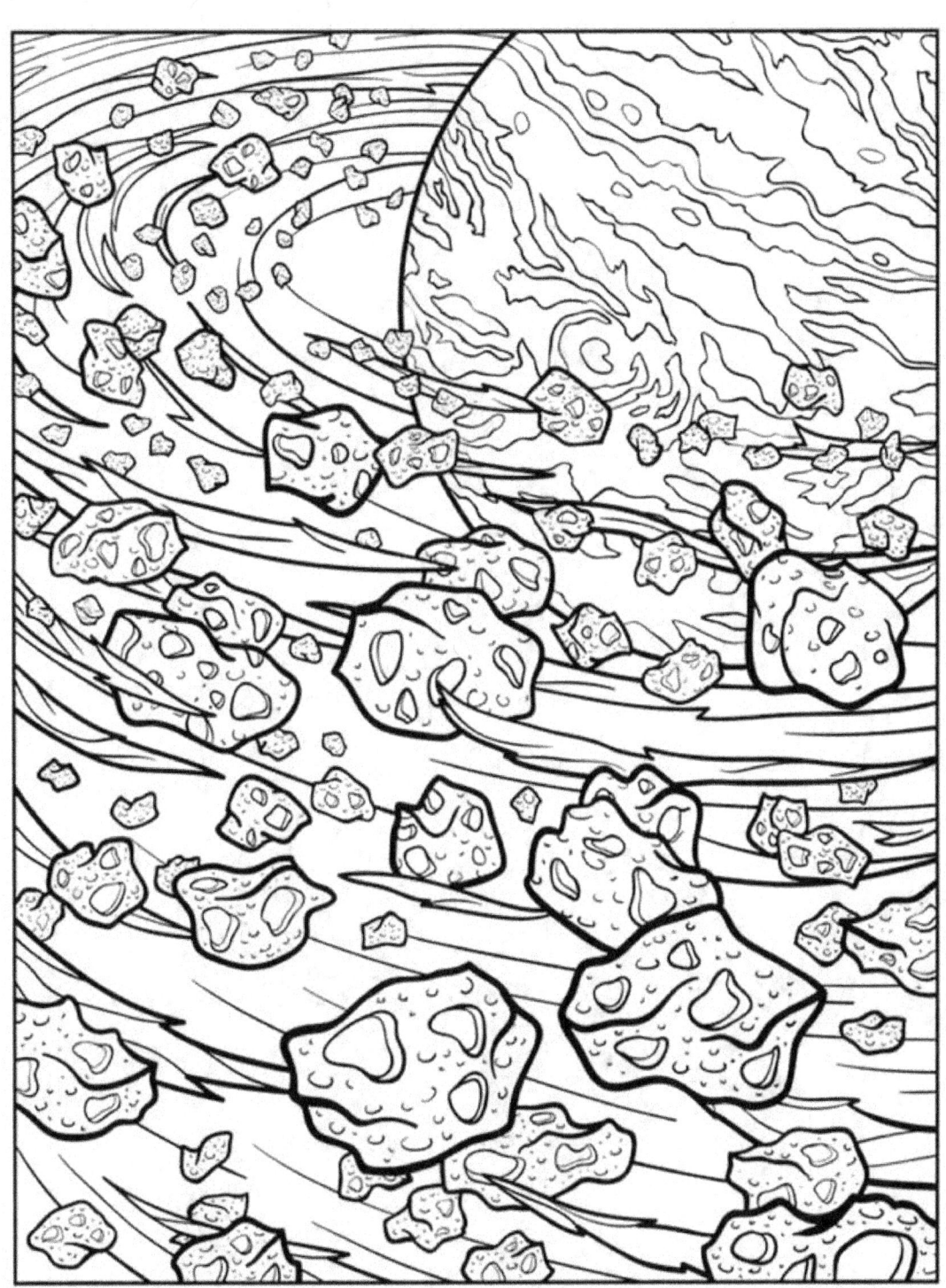

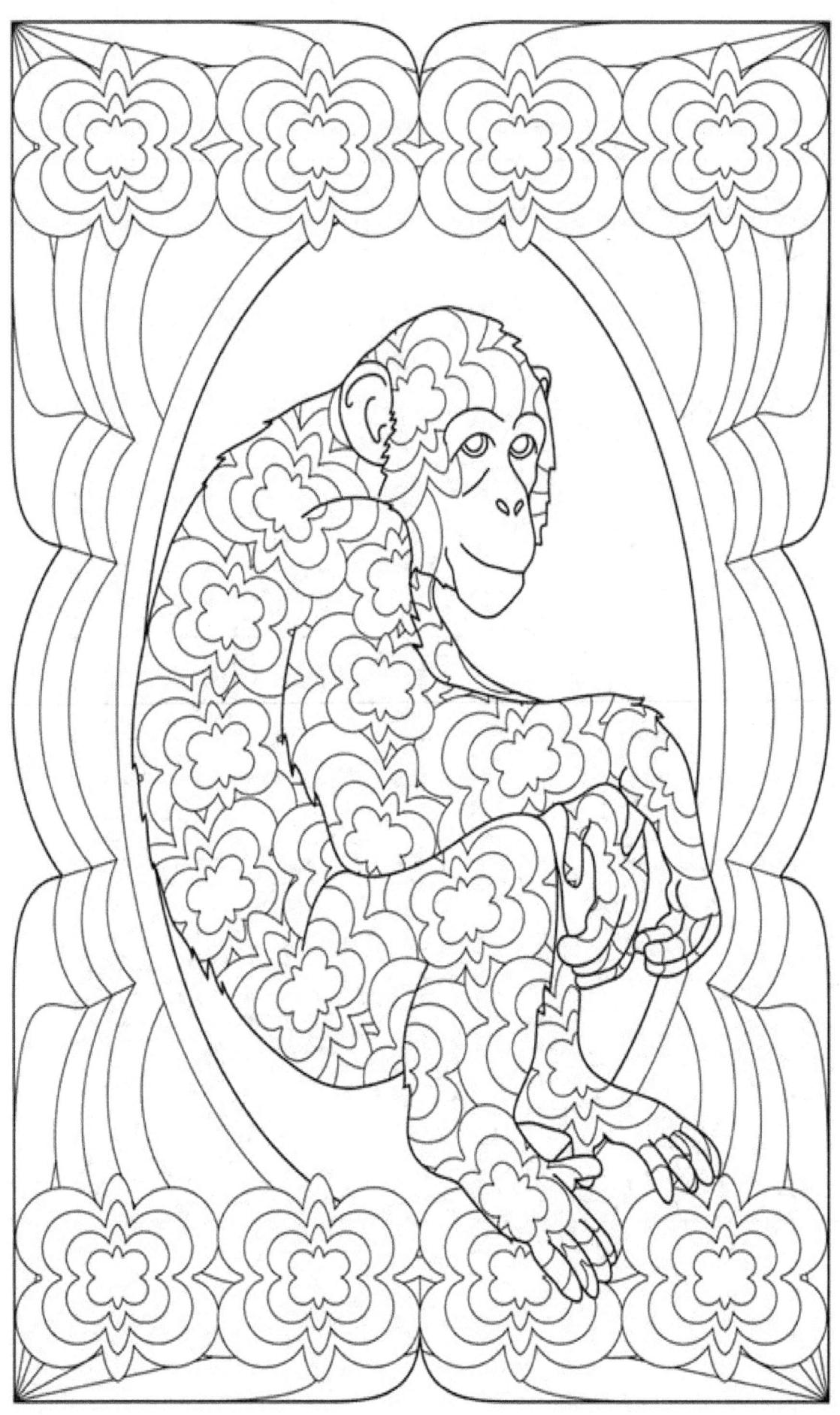

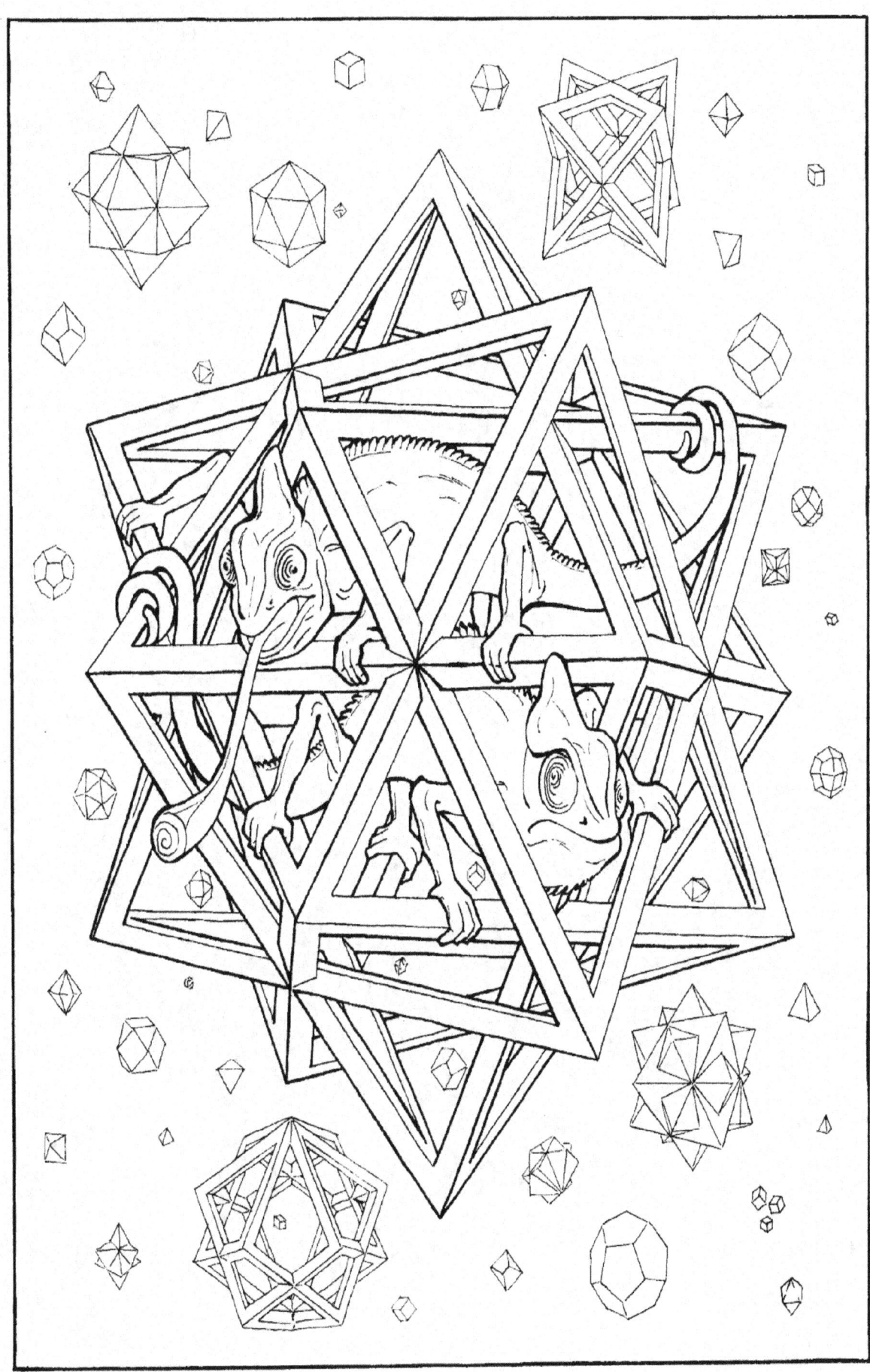

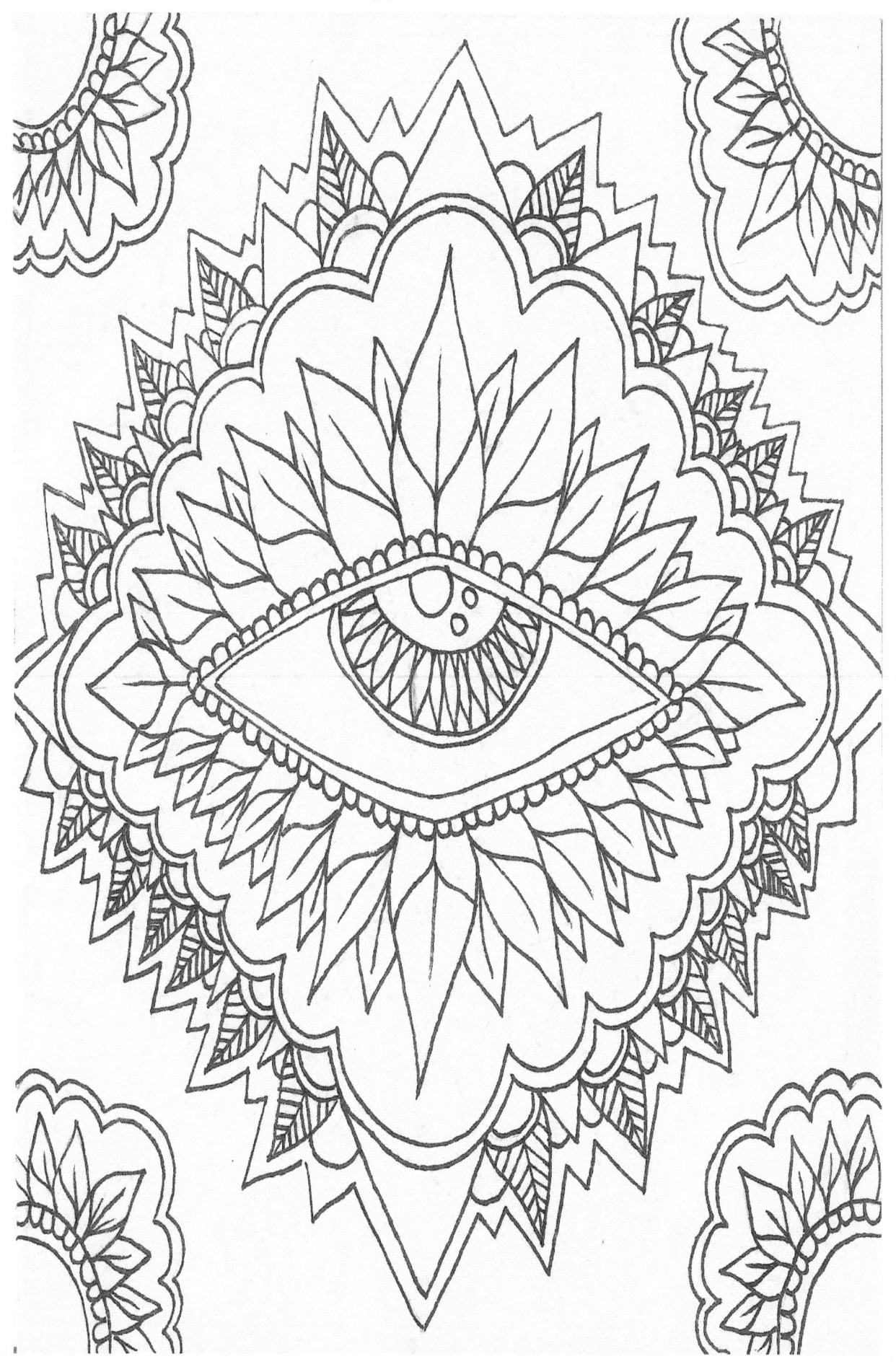

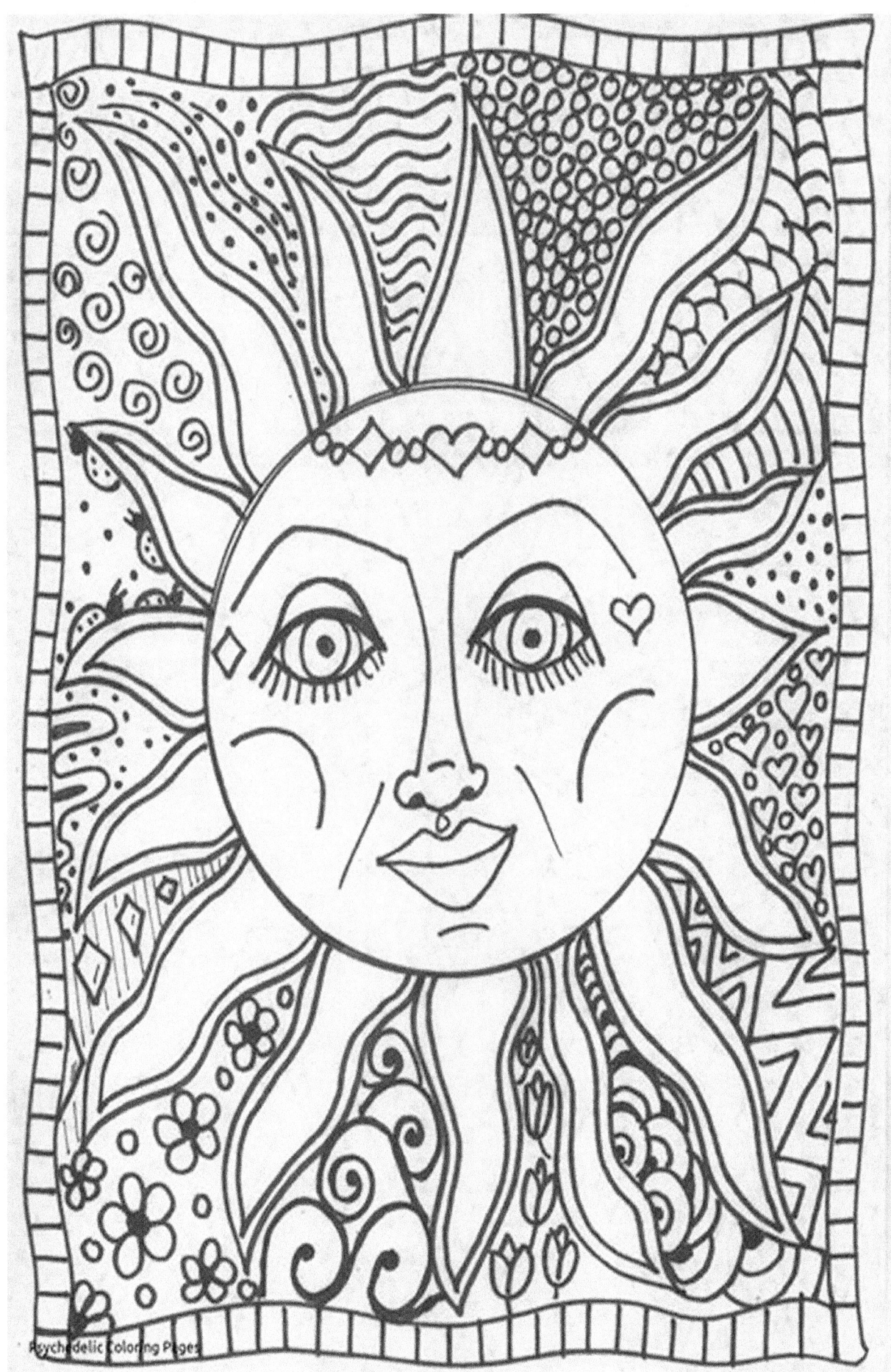

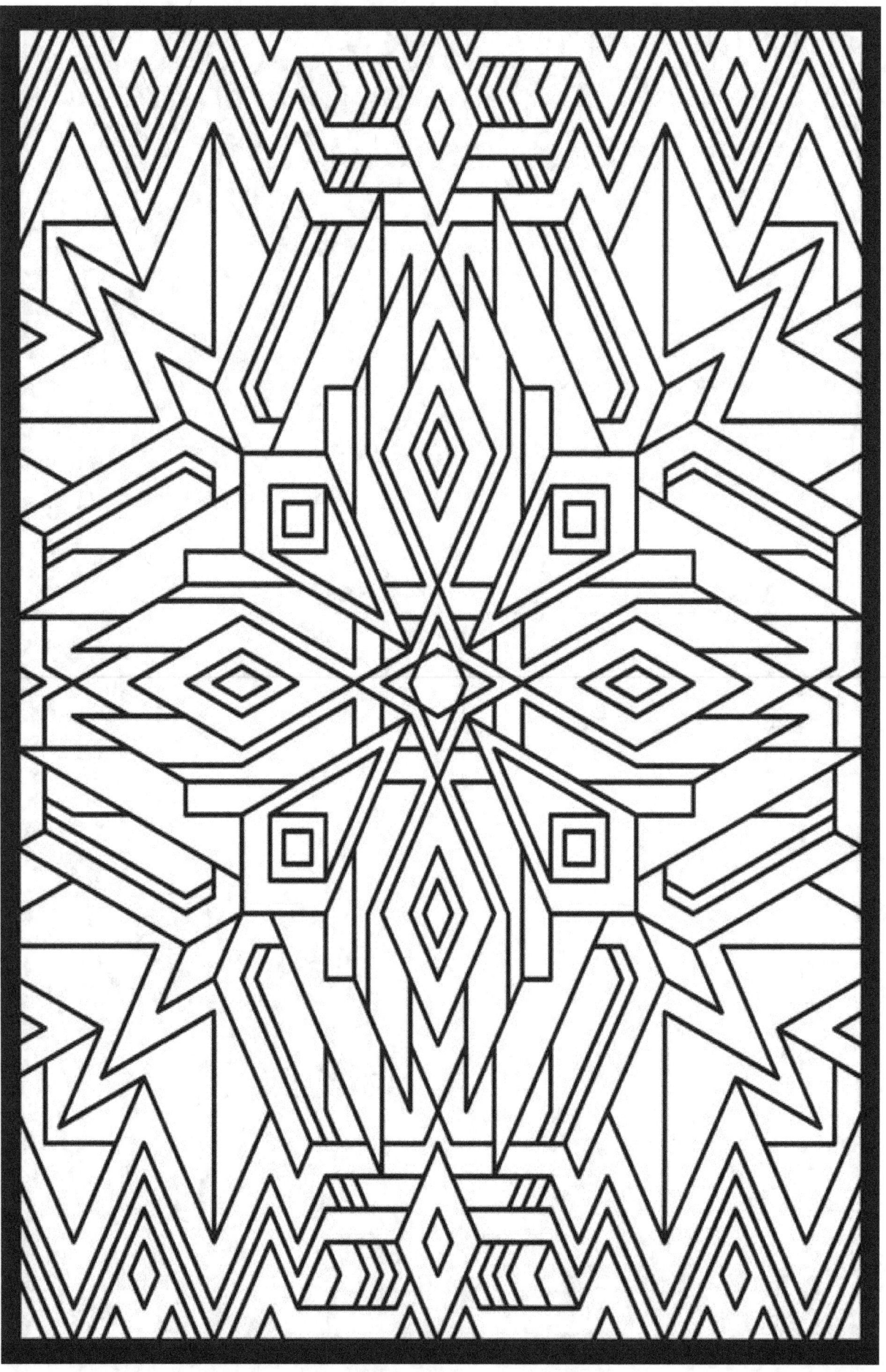

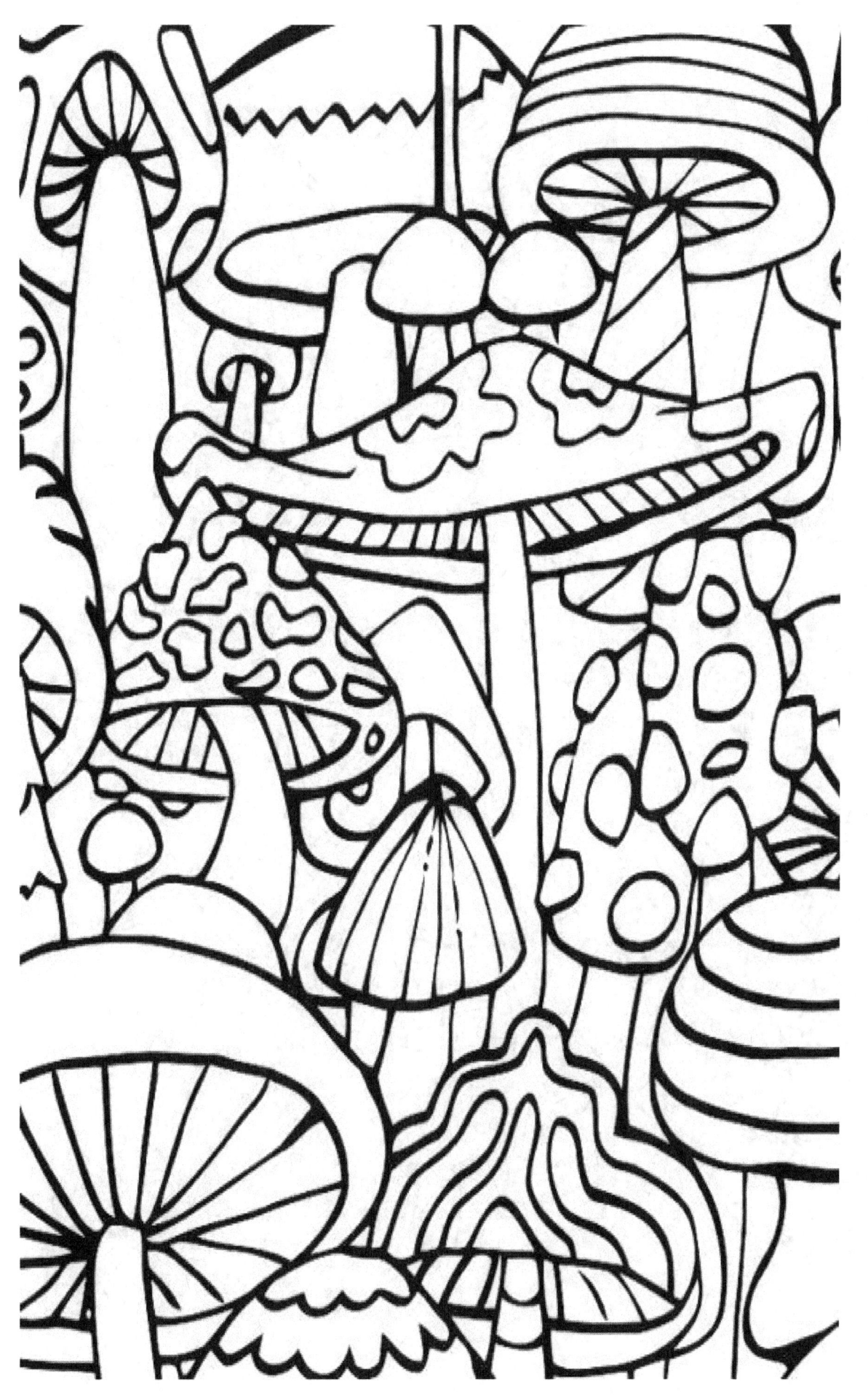

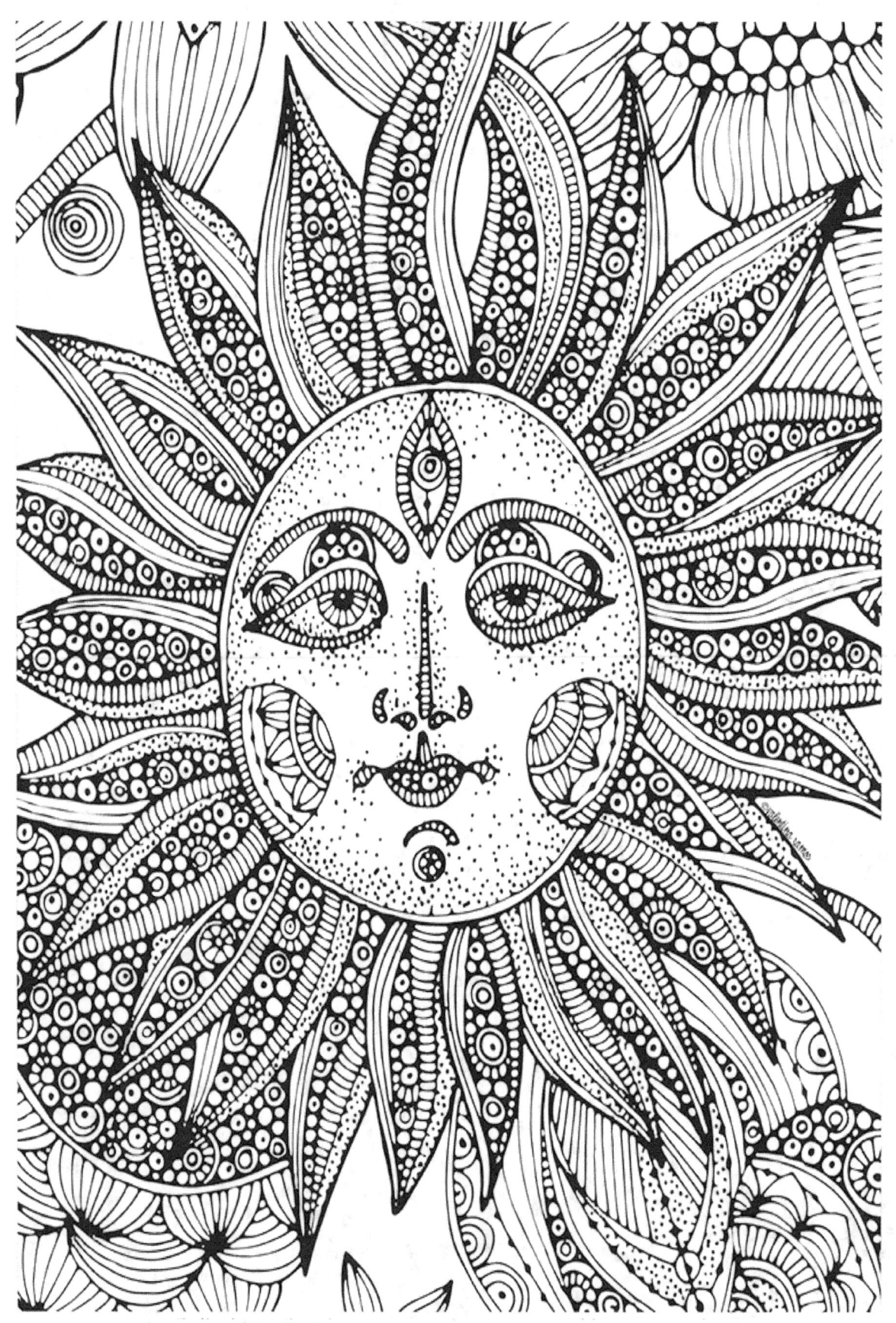

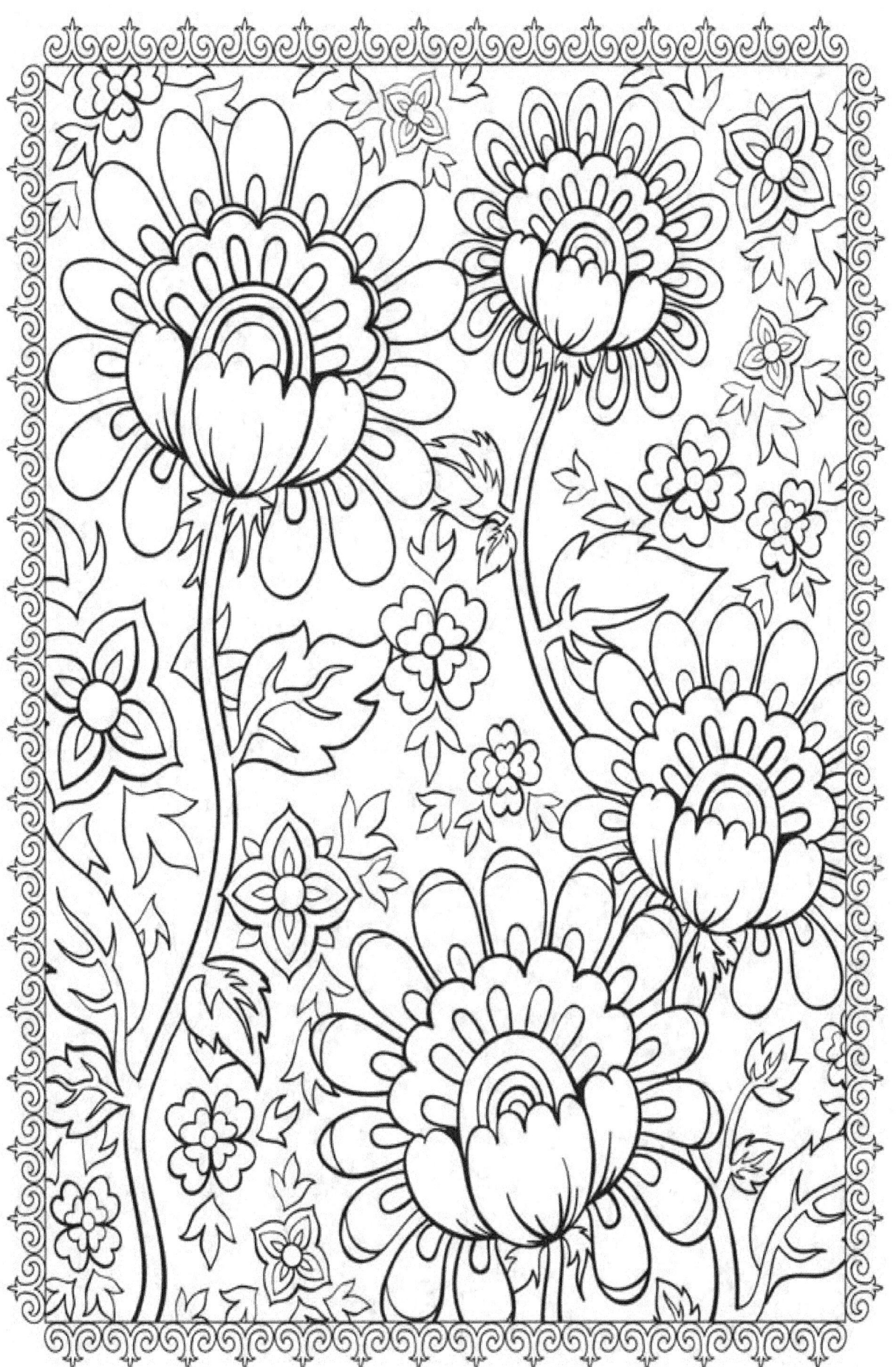

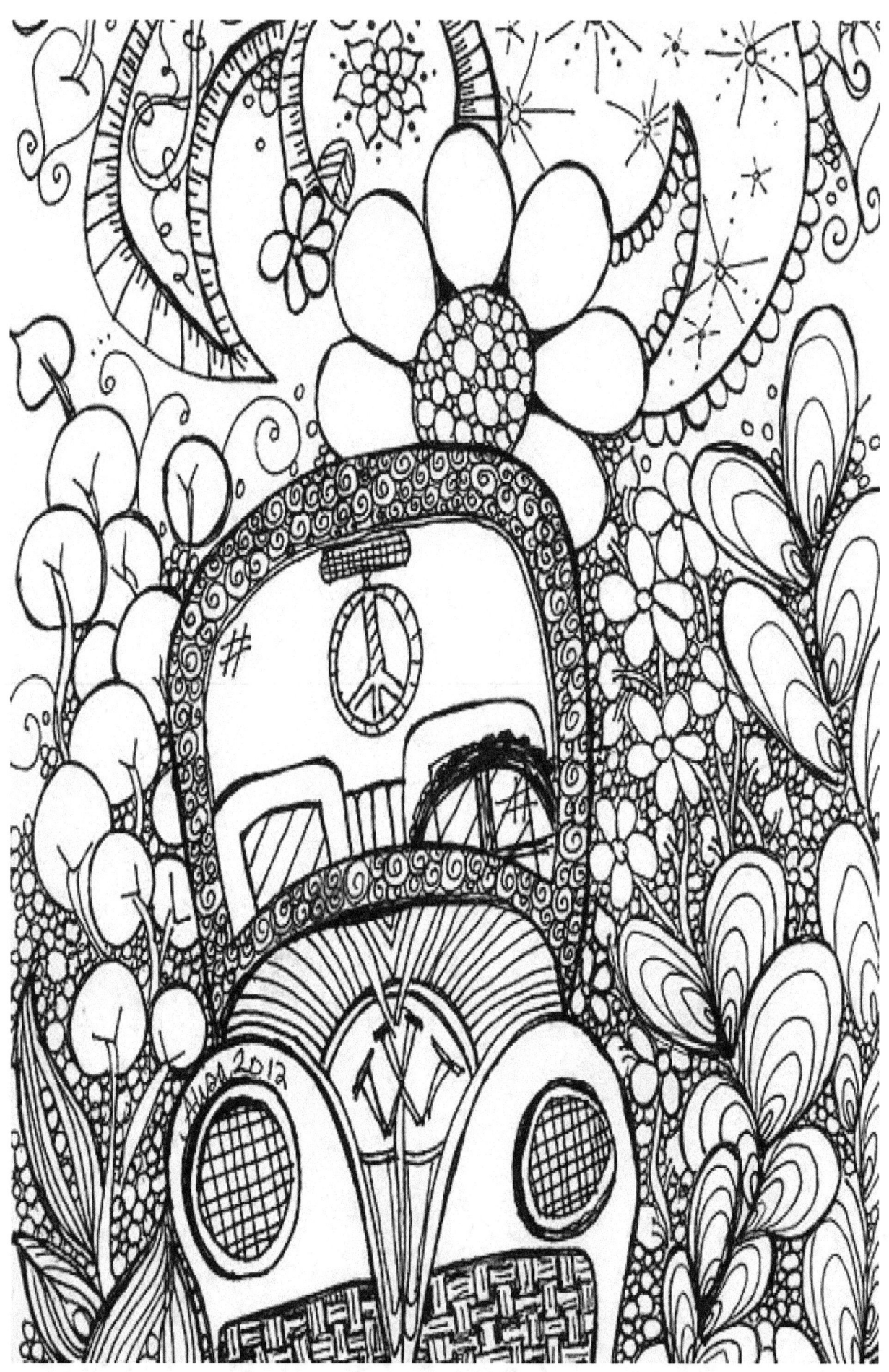

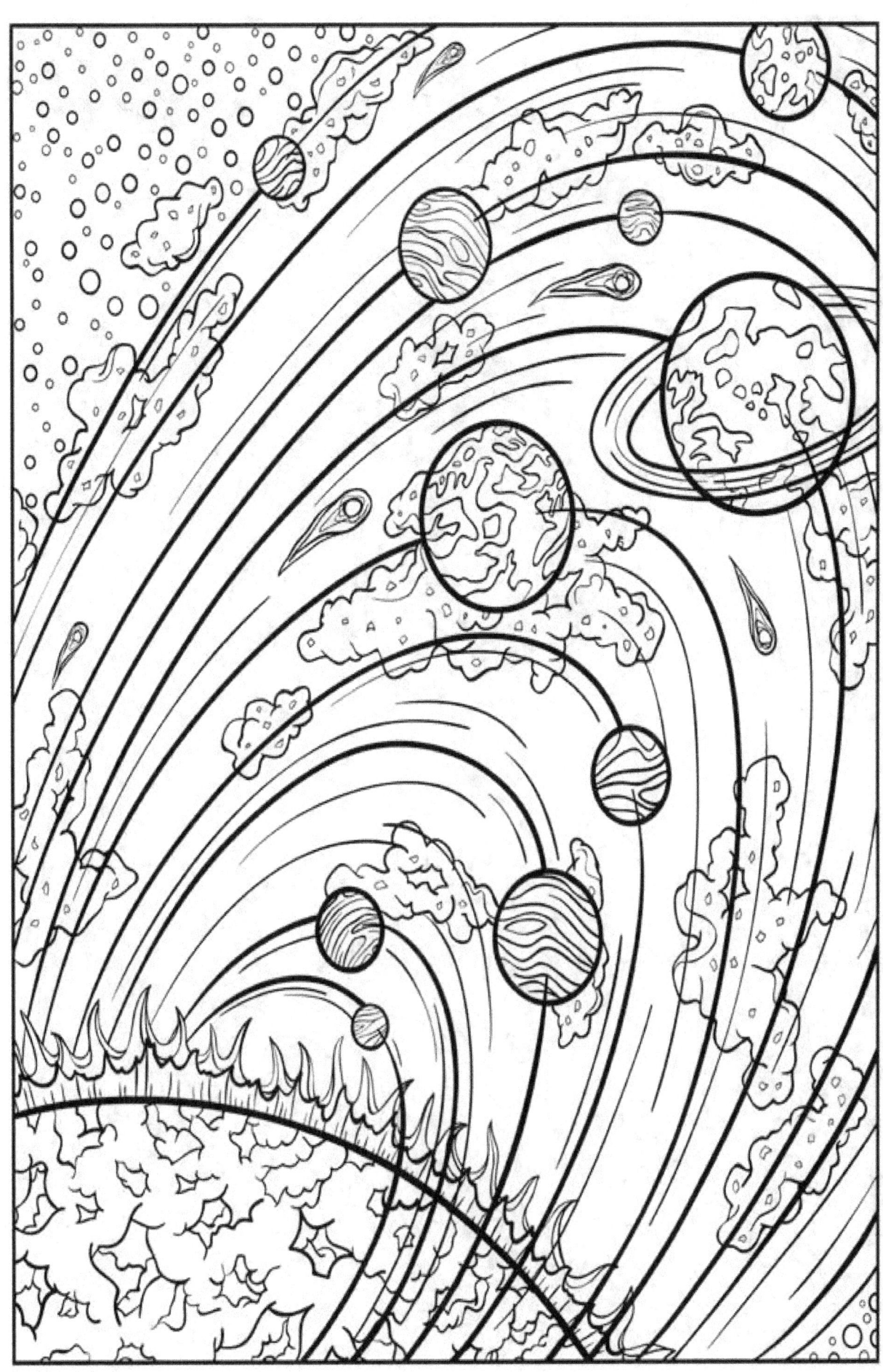

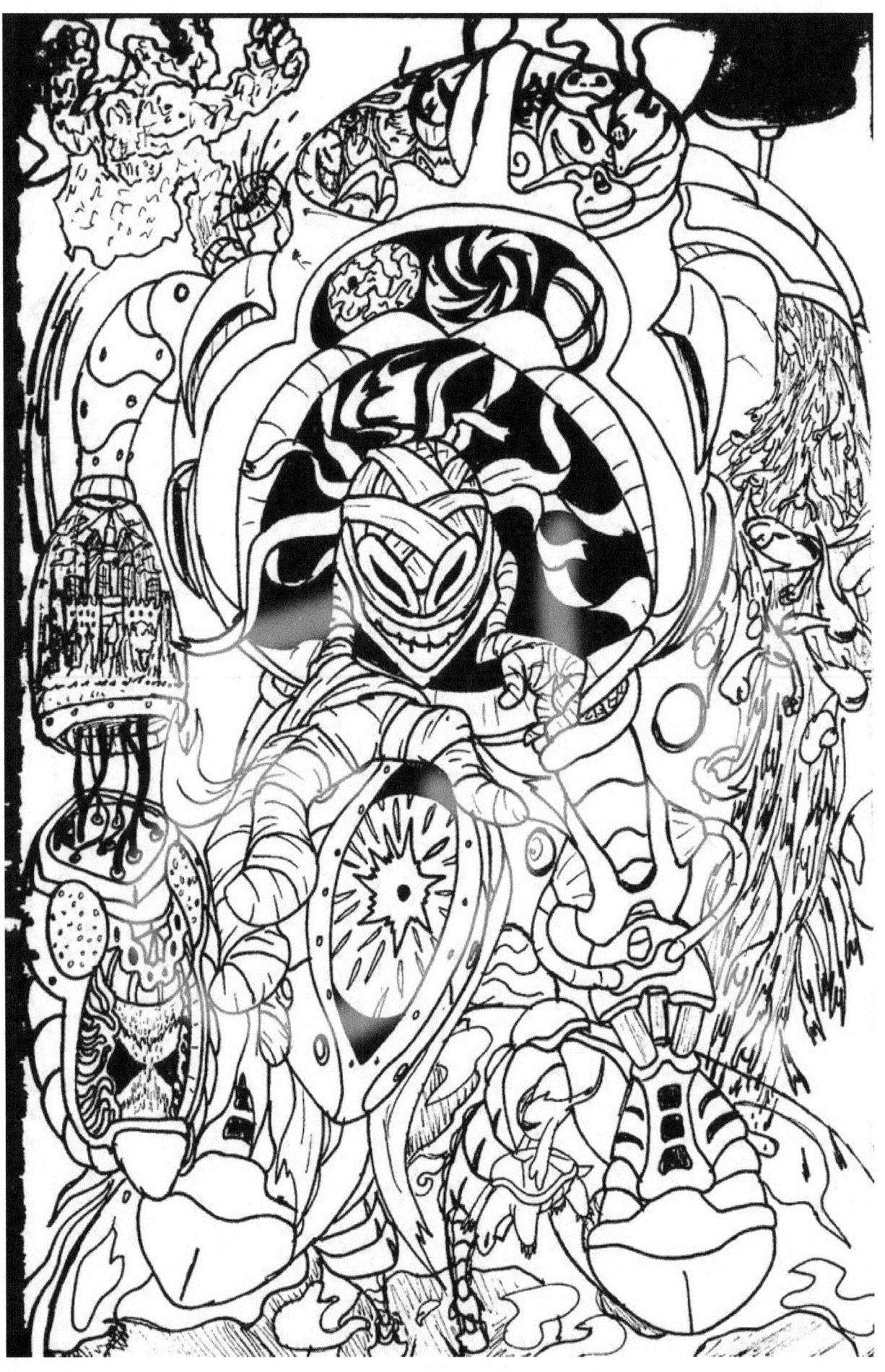

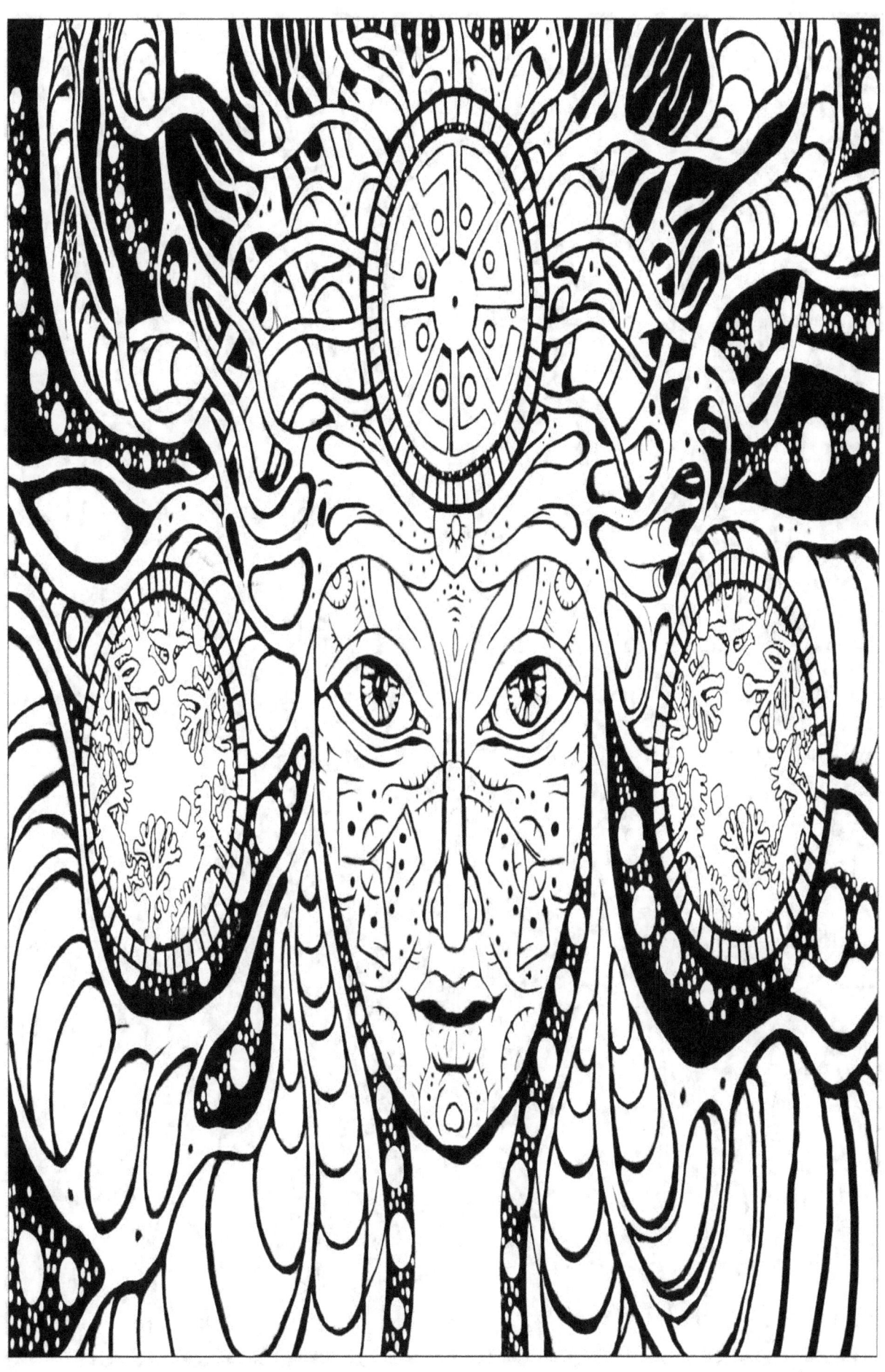

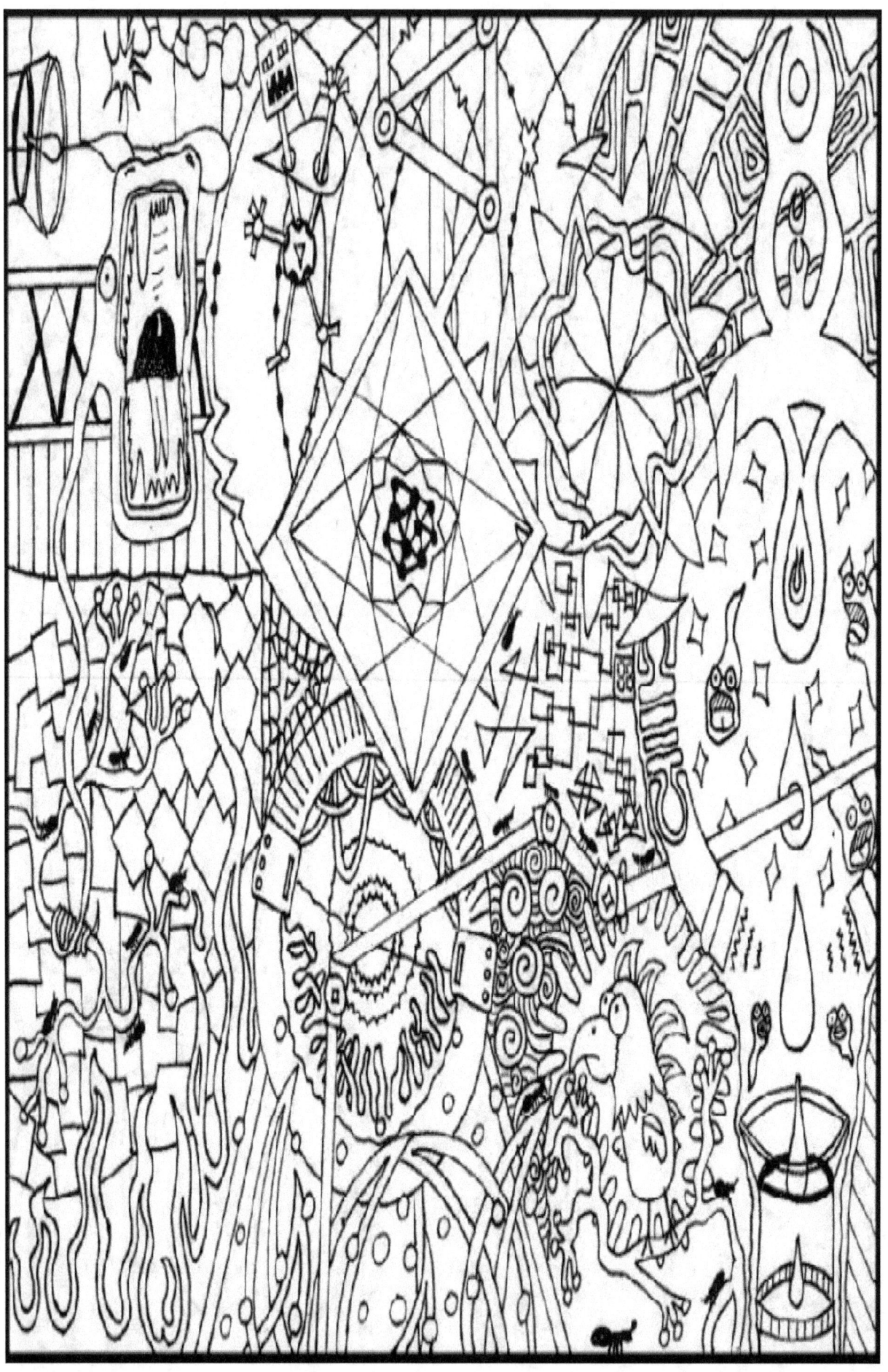

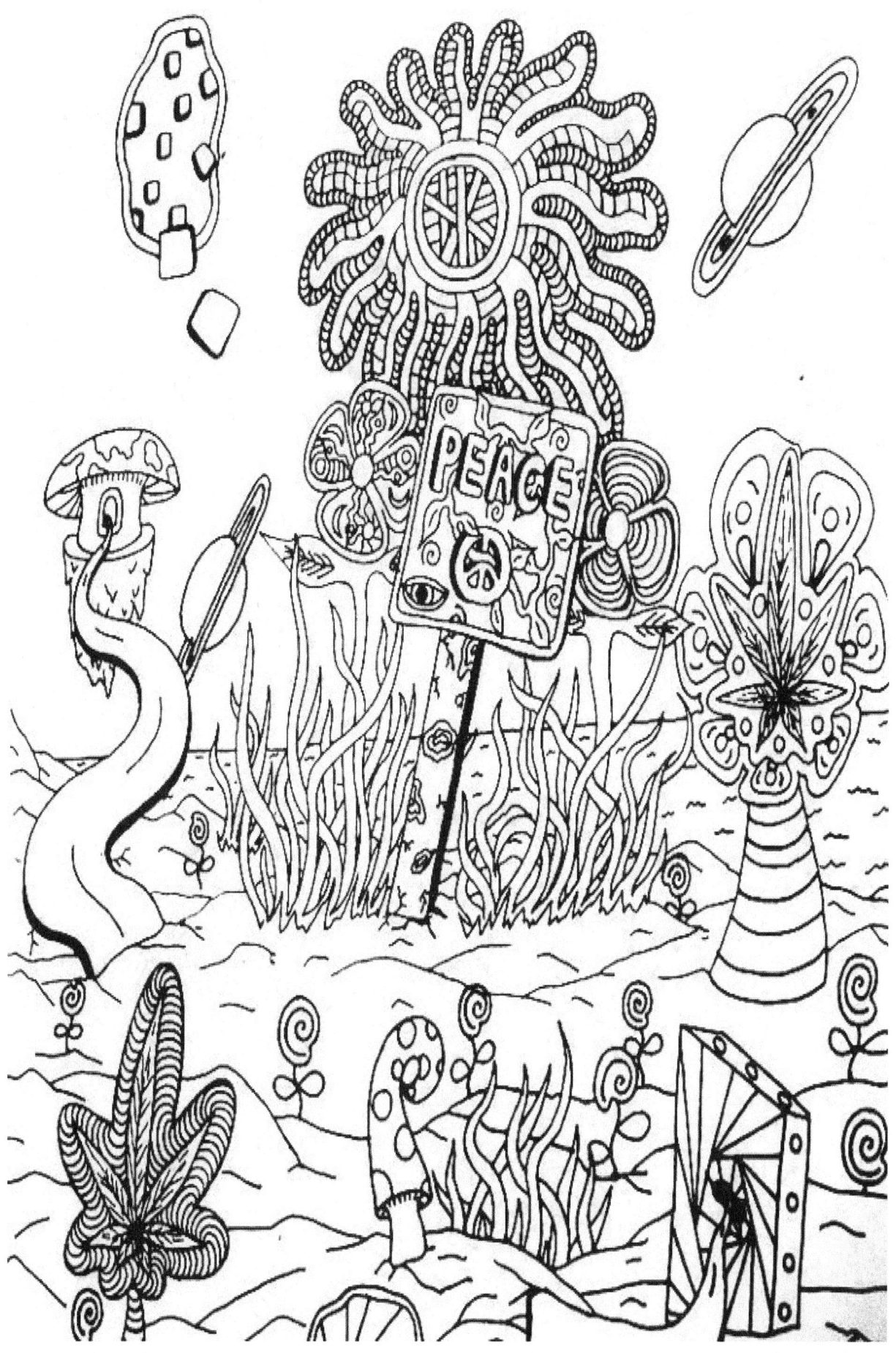

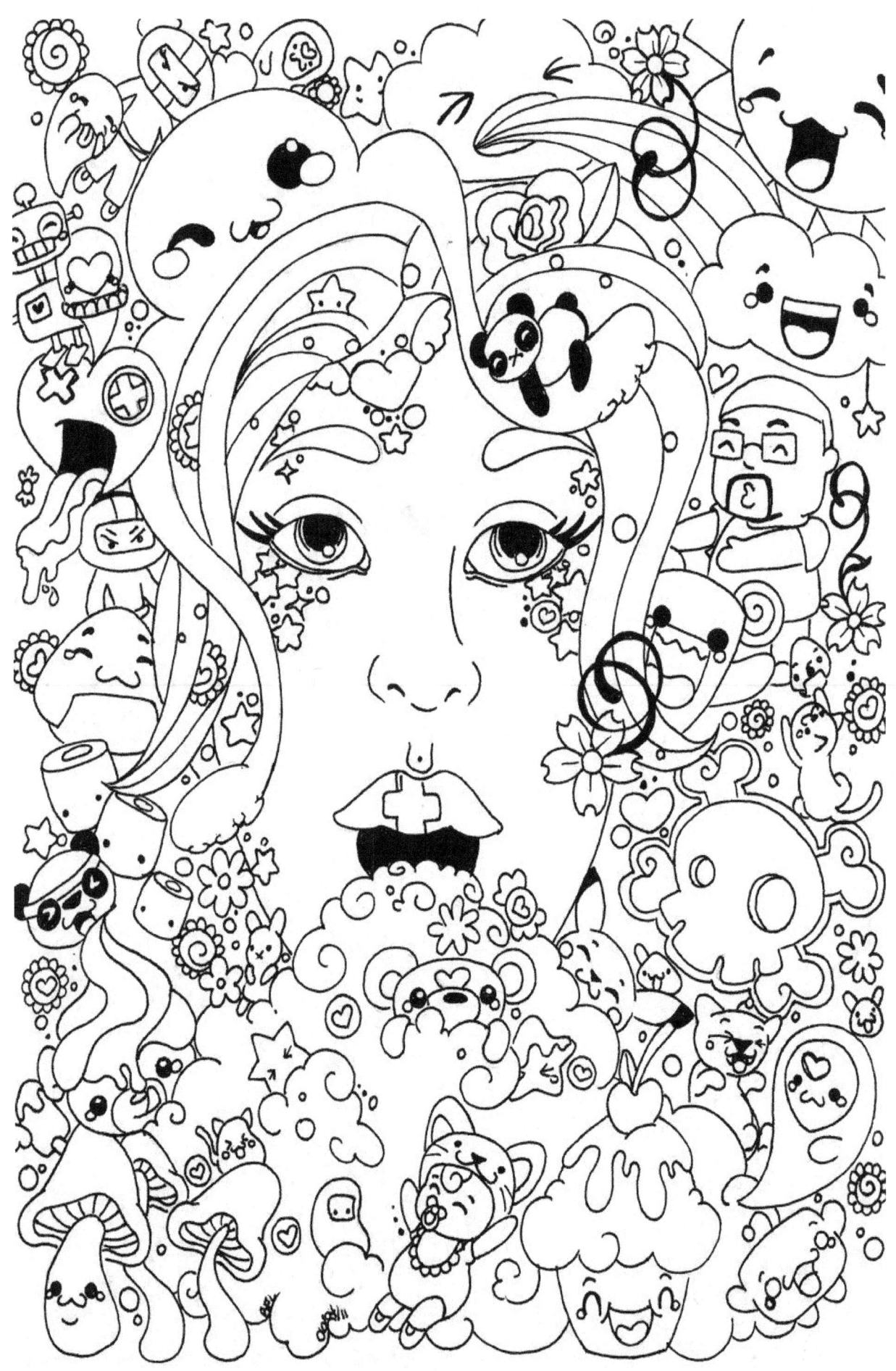

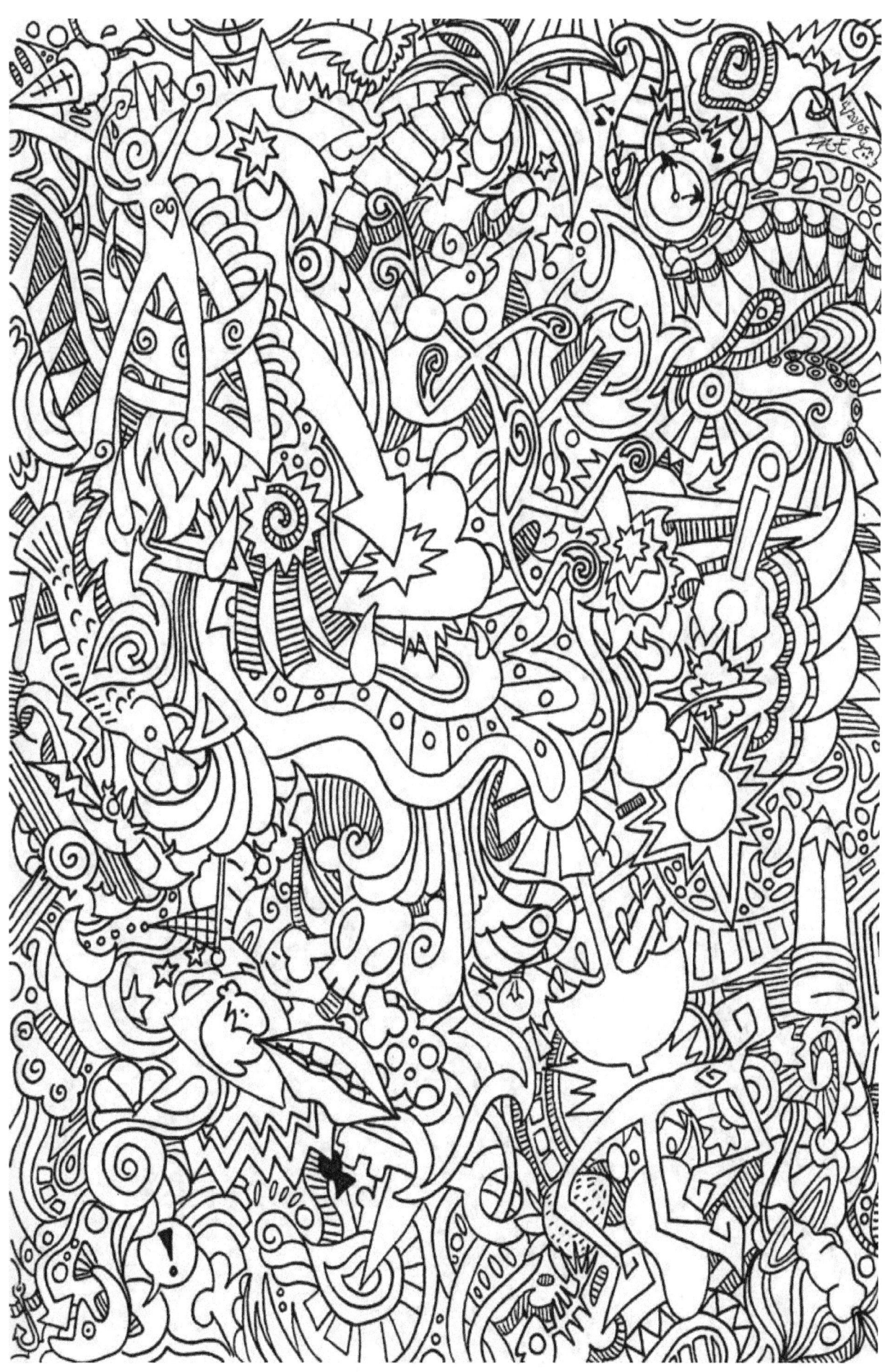

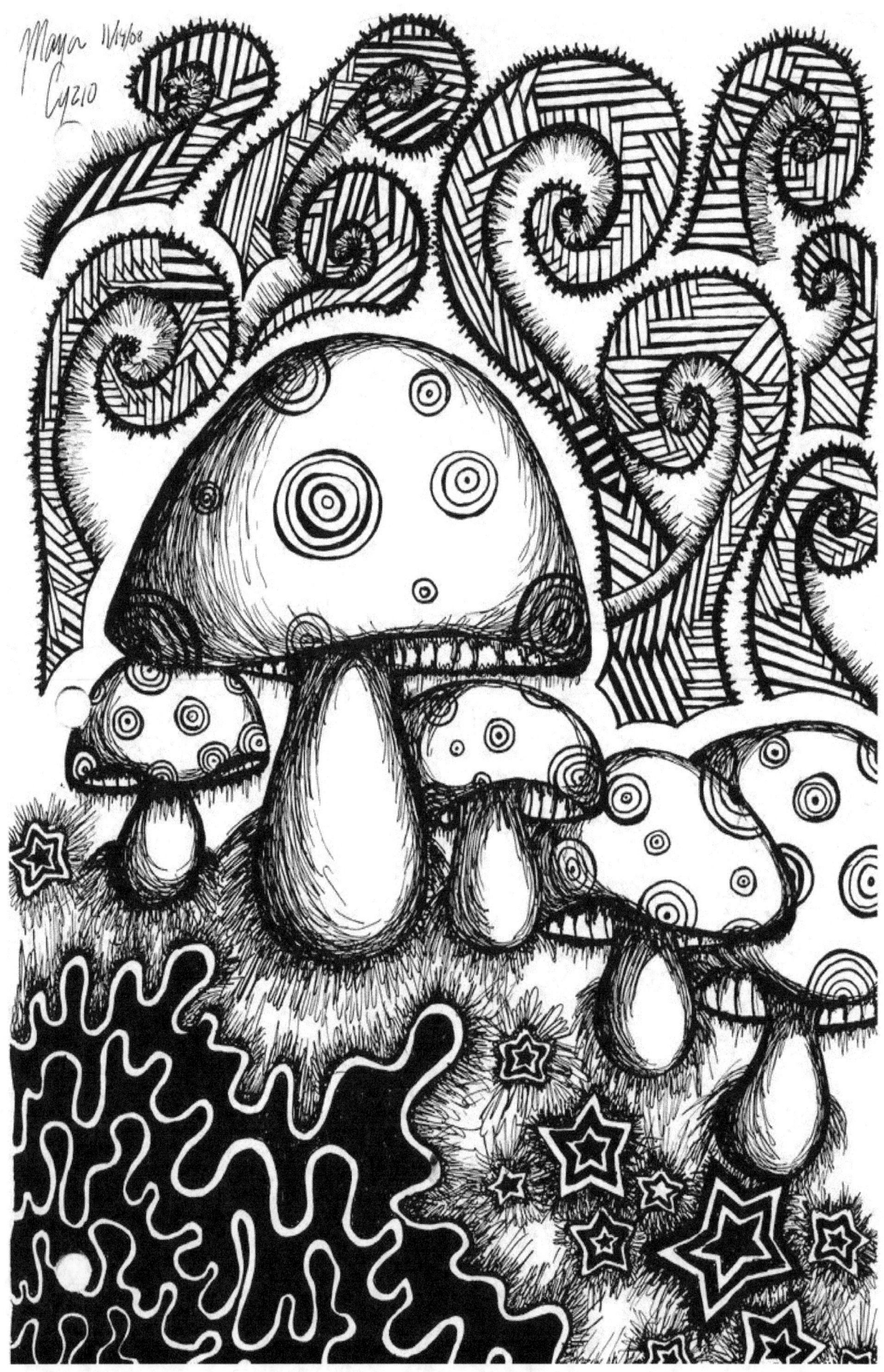

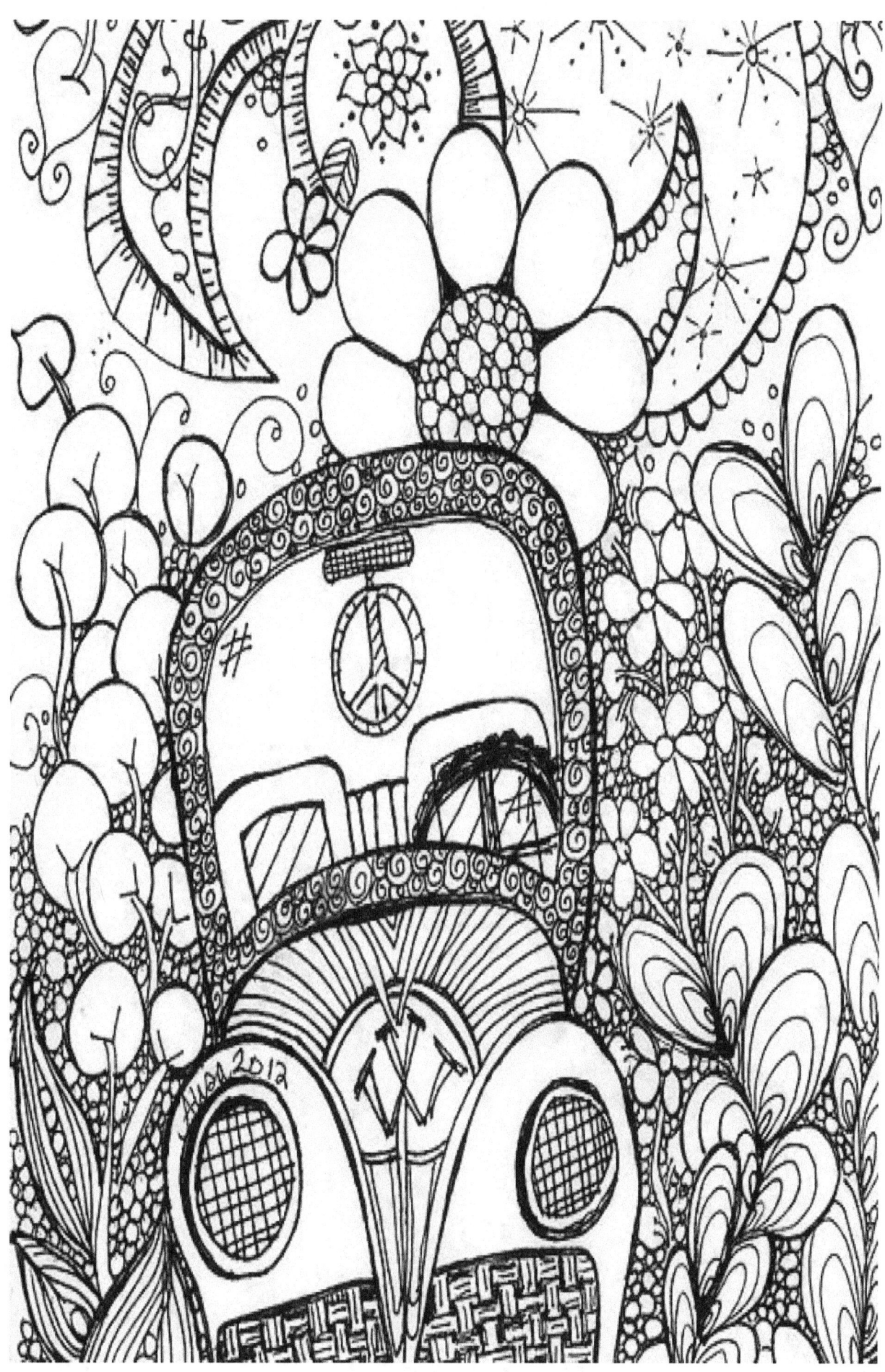

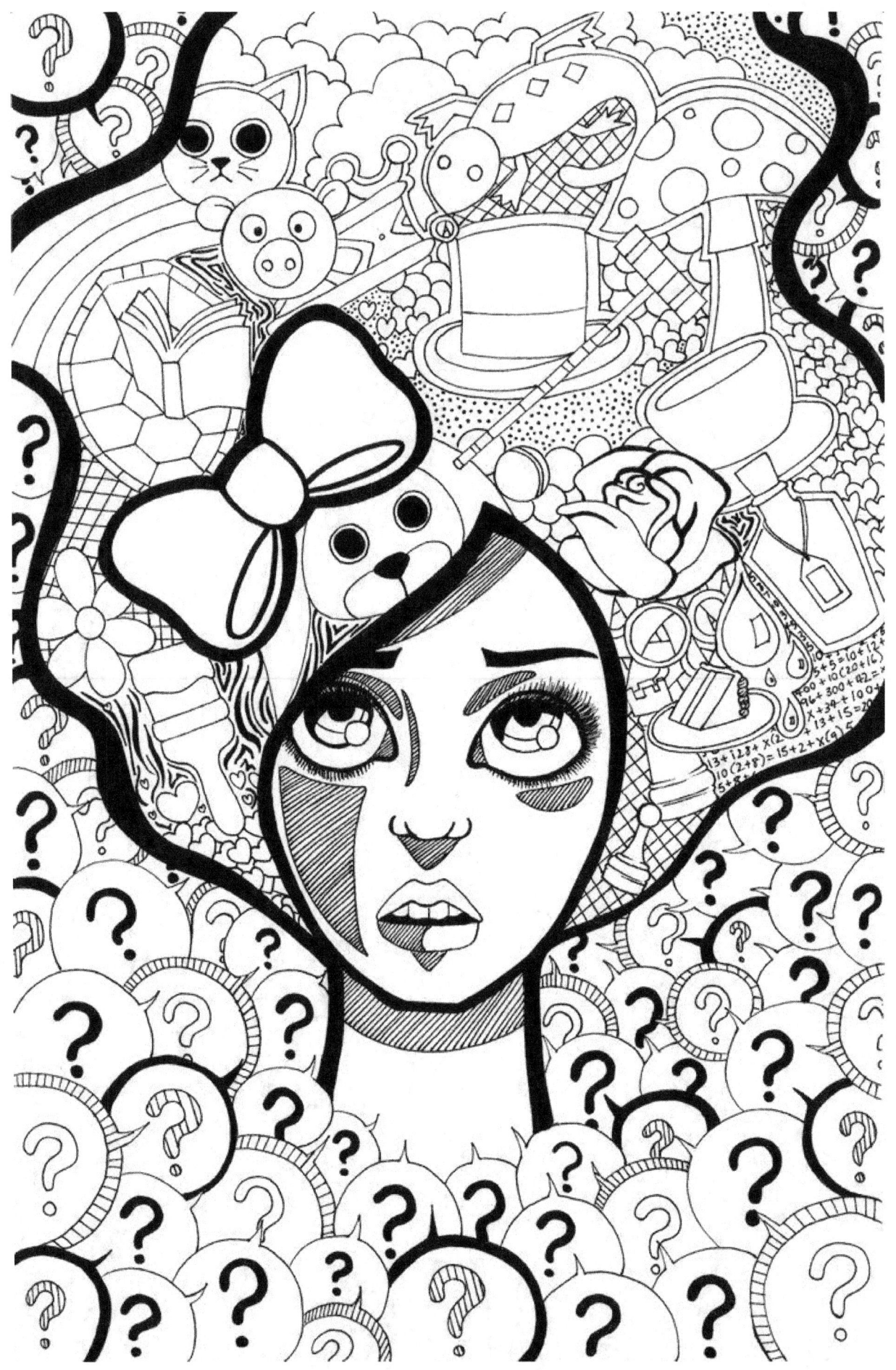

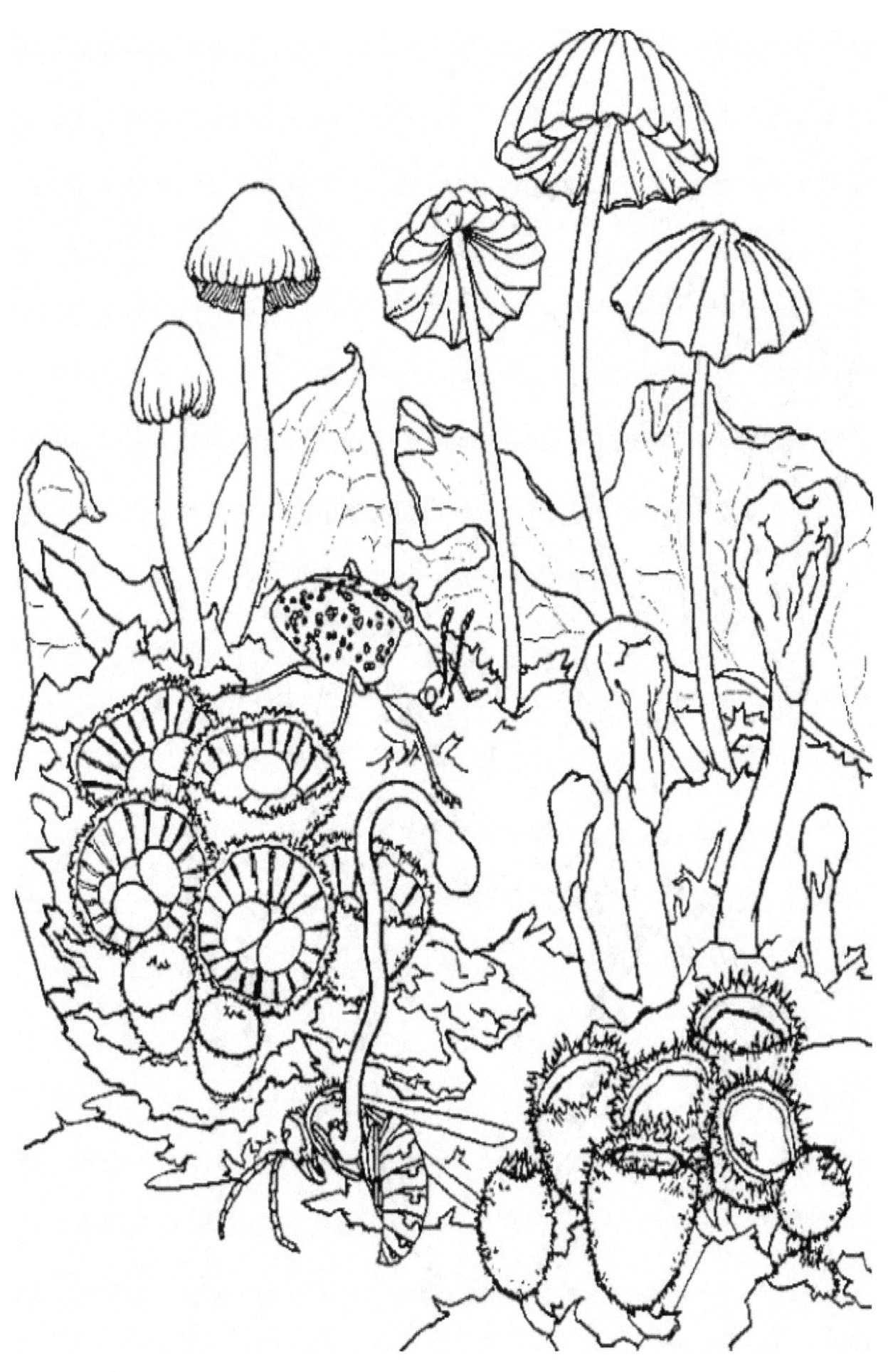

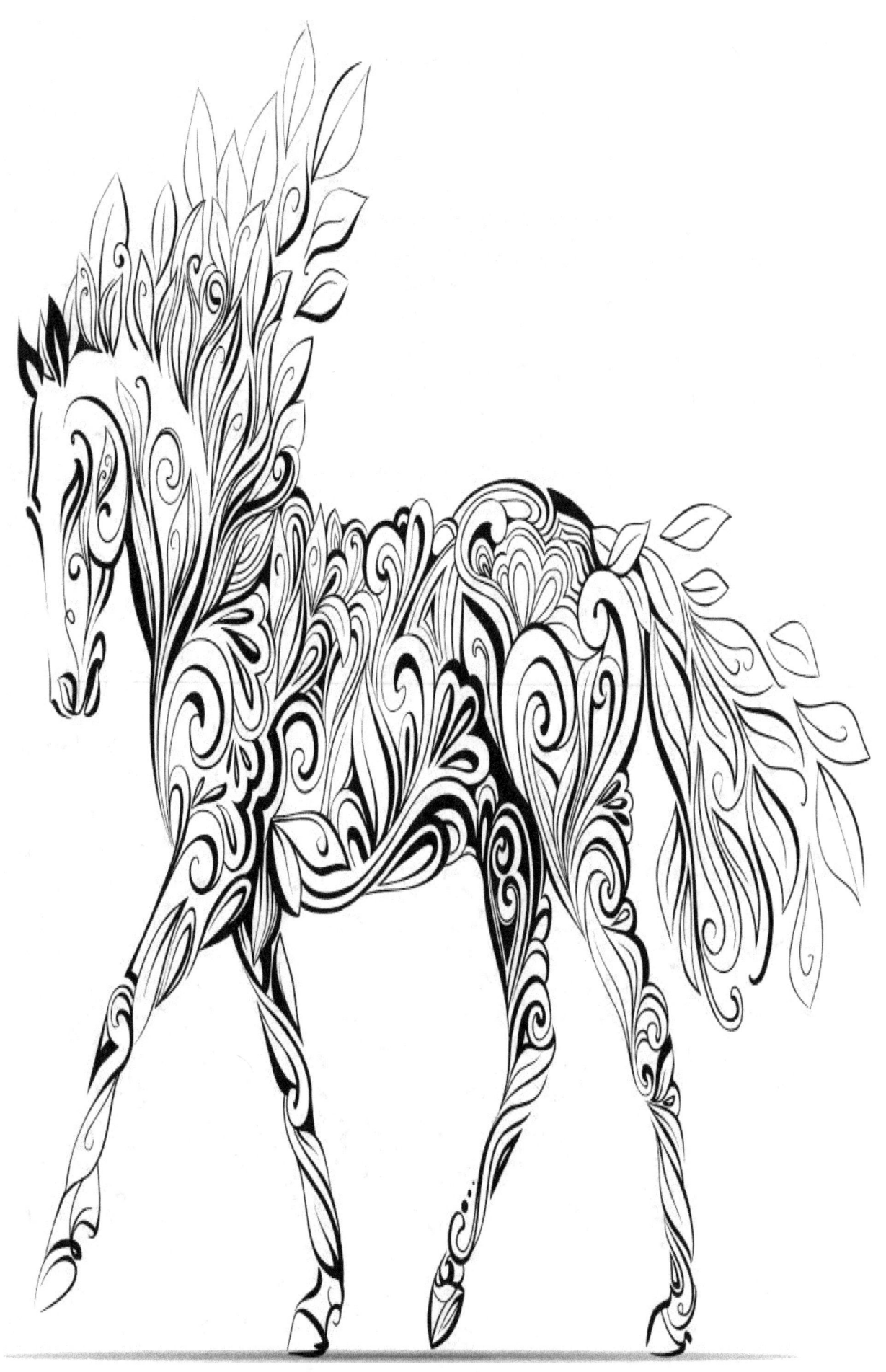

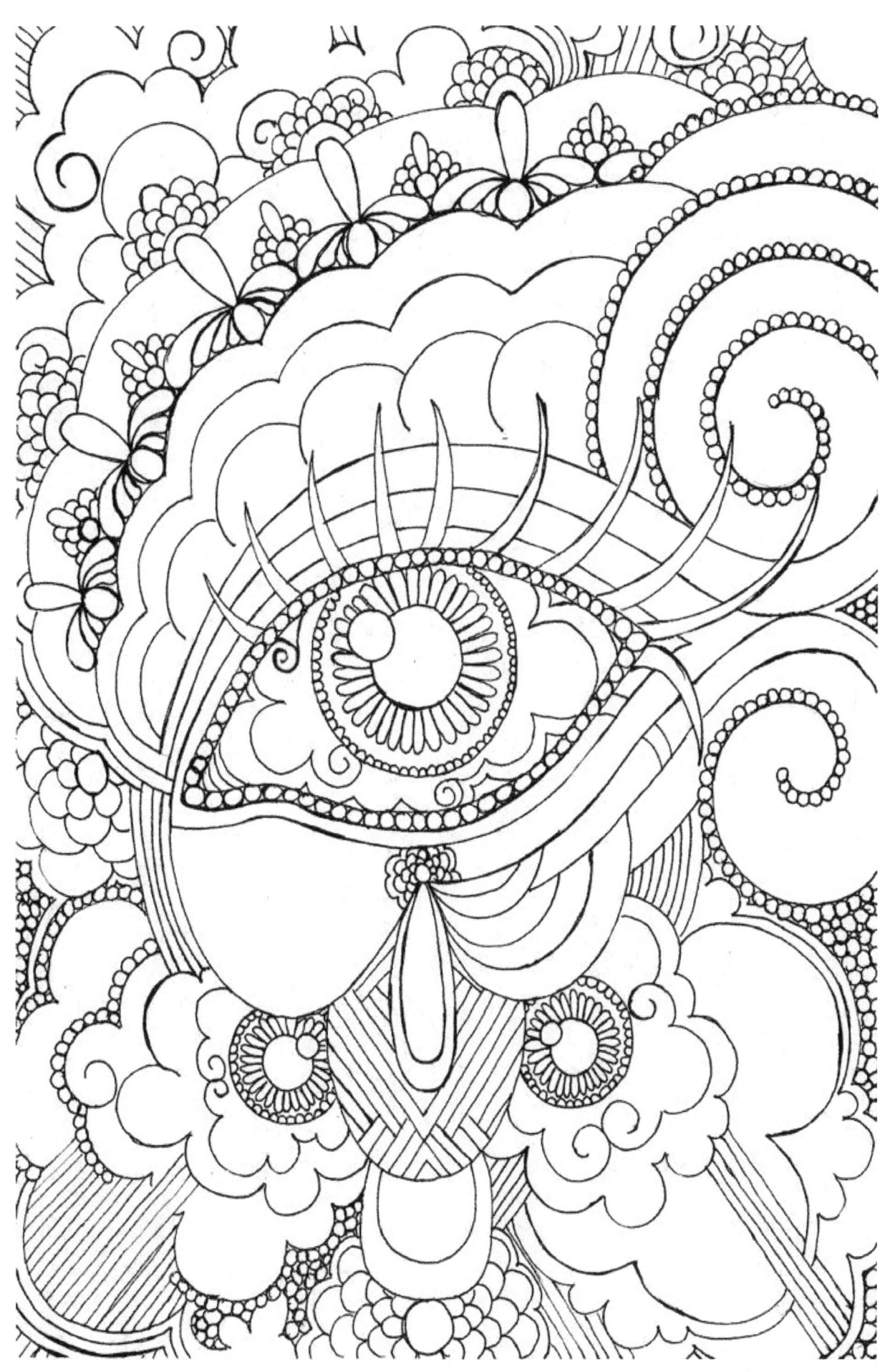

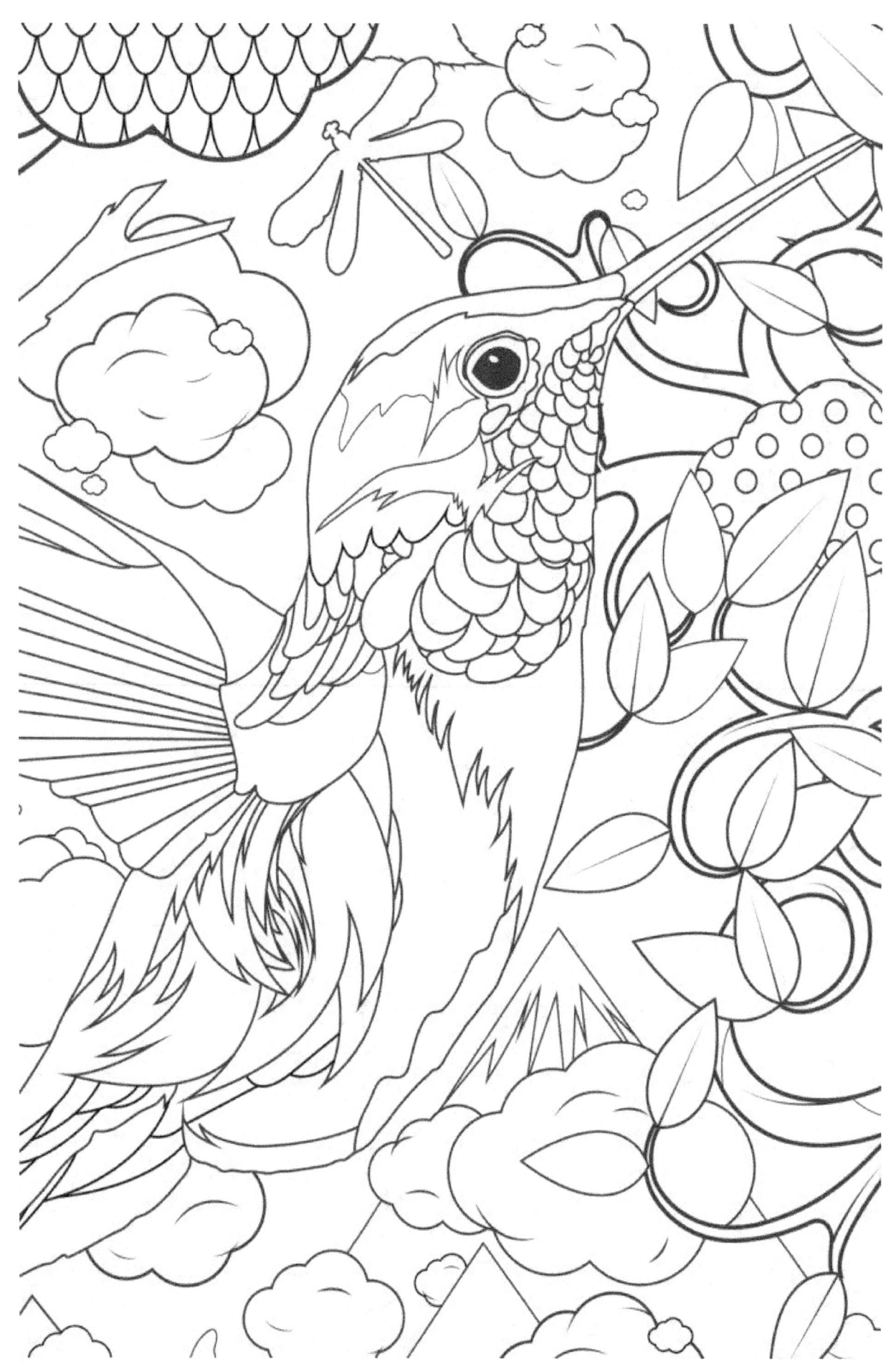

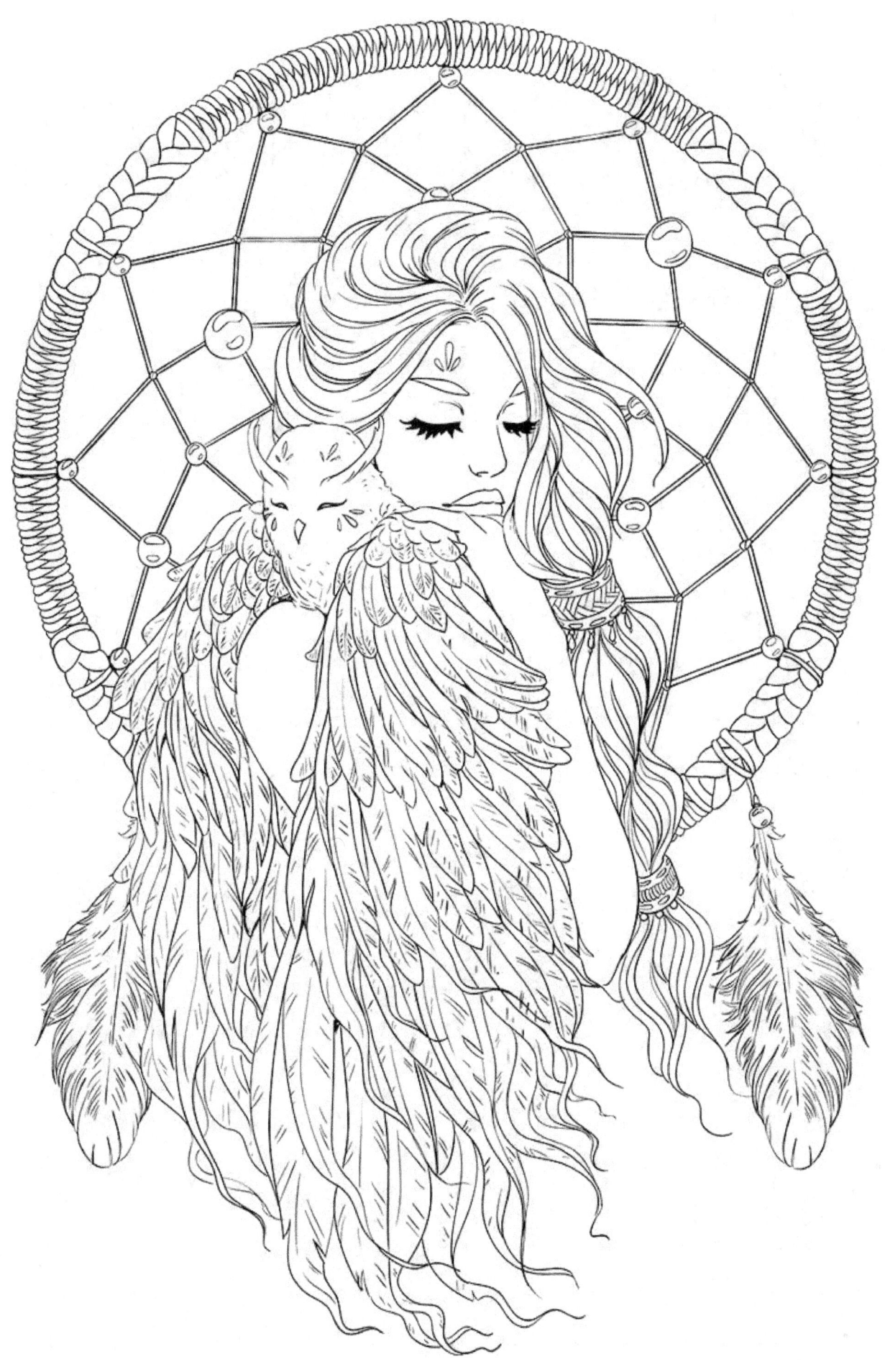

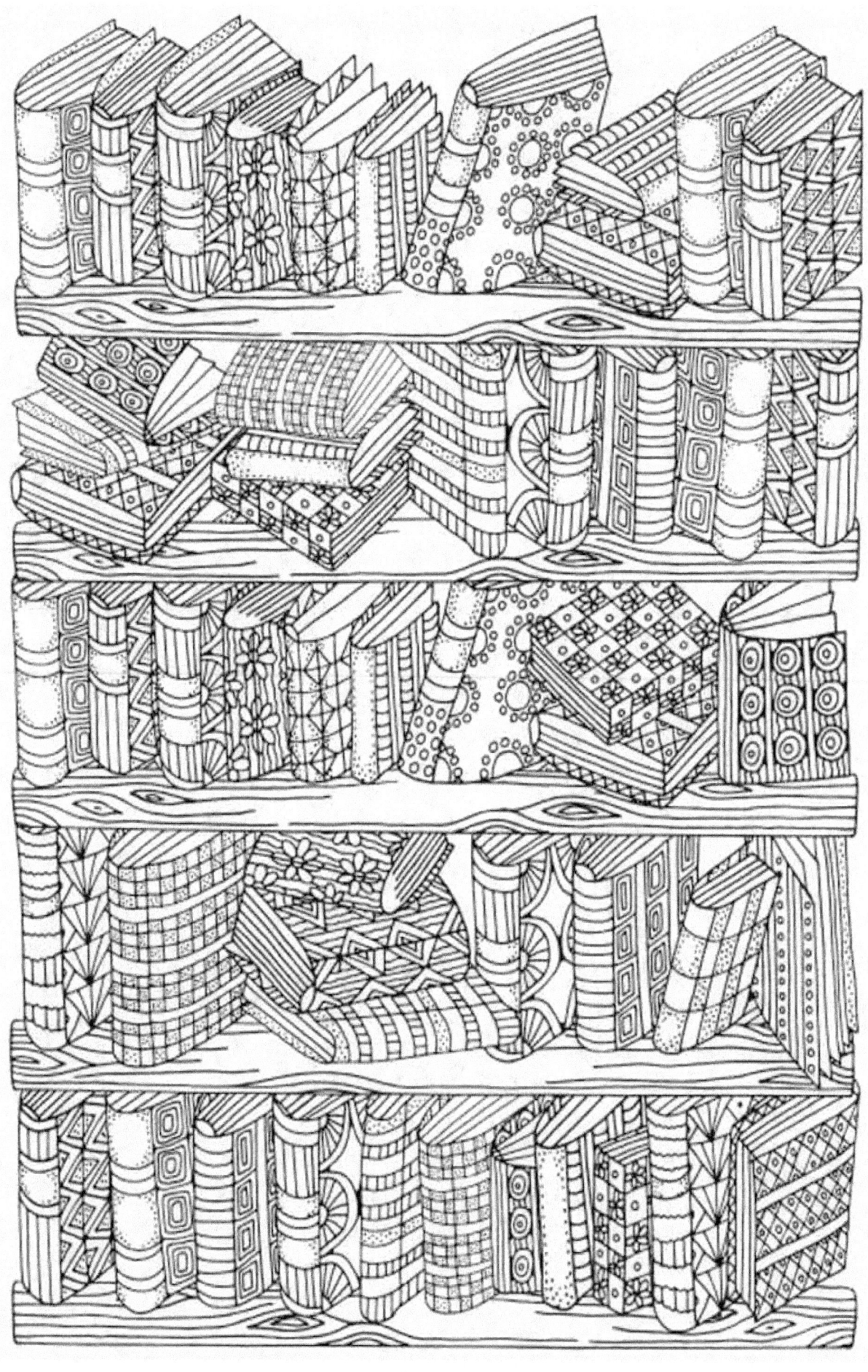

vv

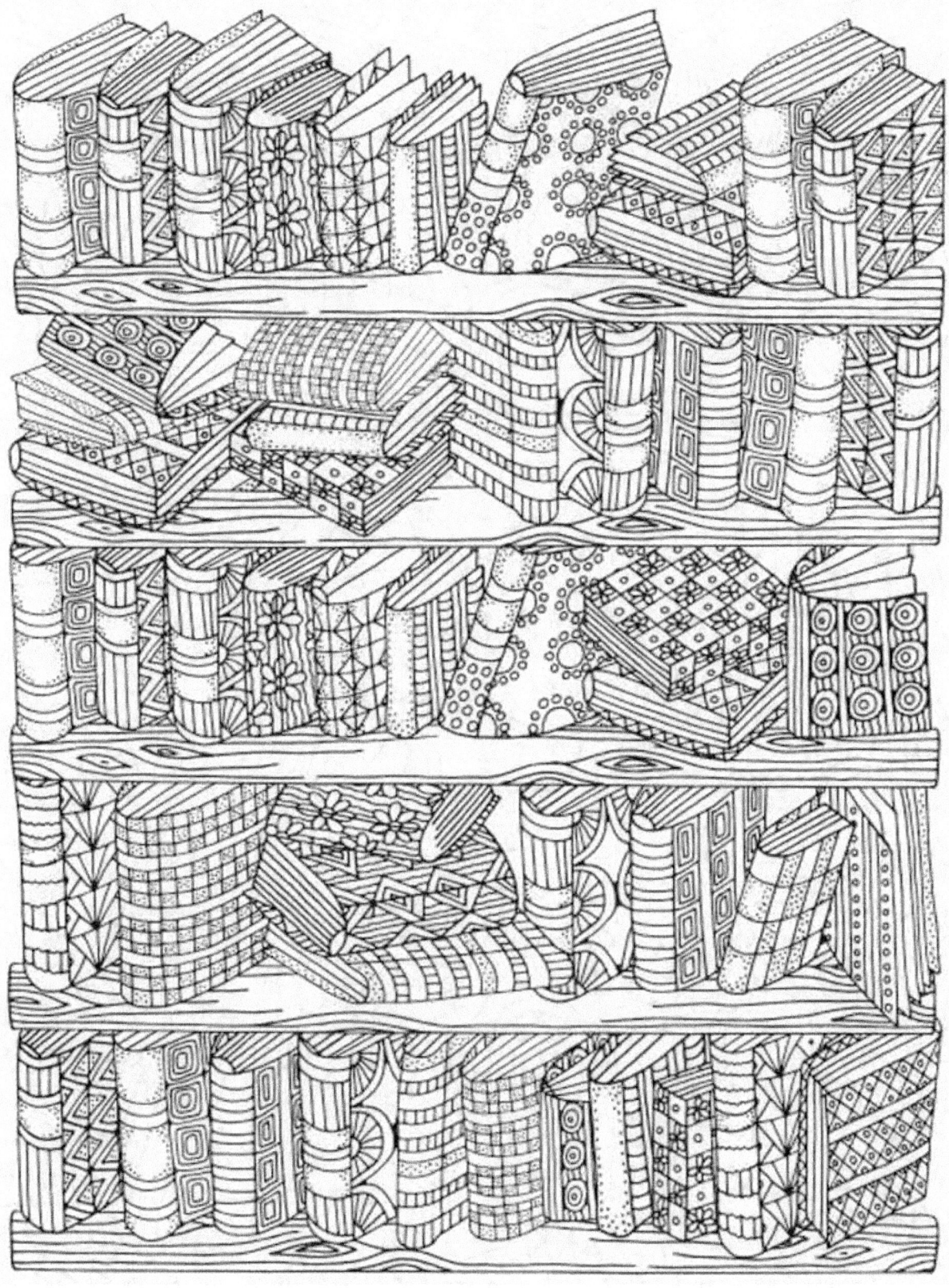

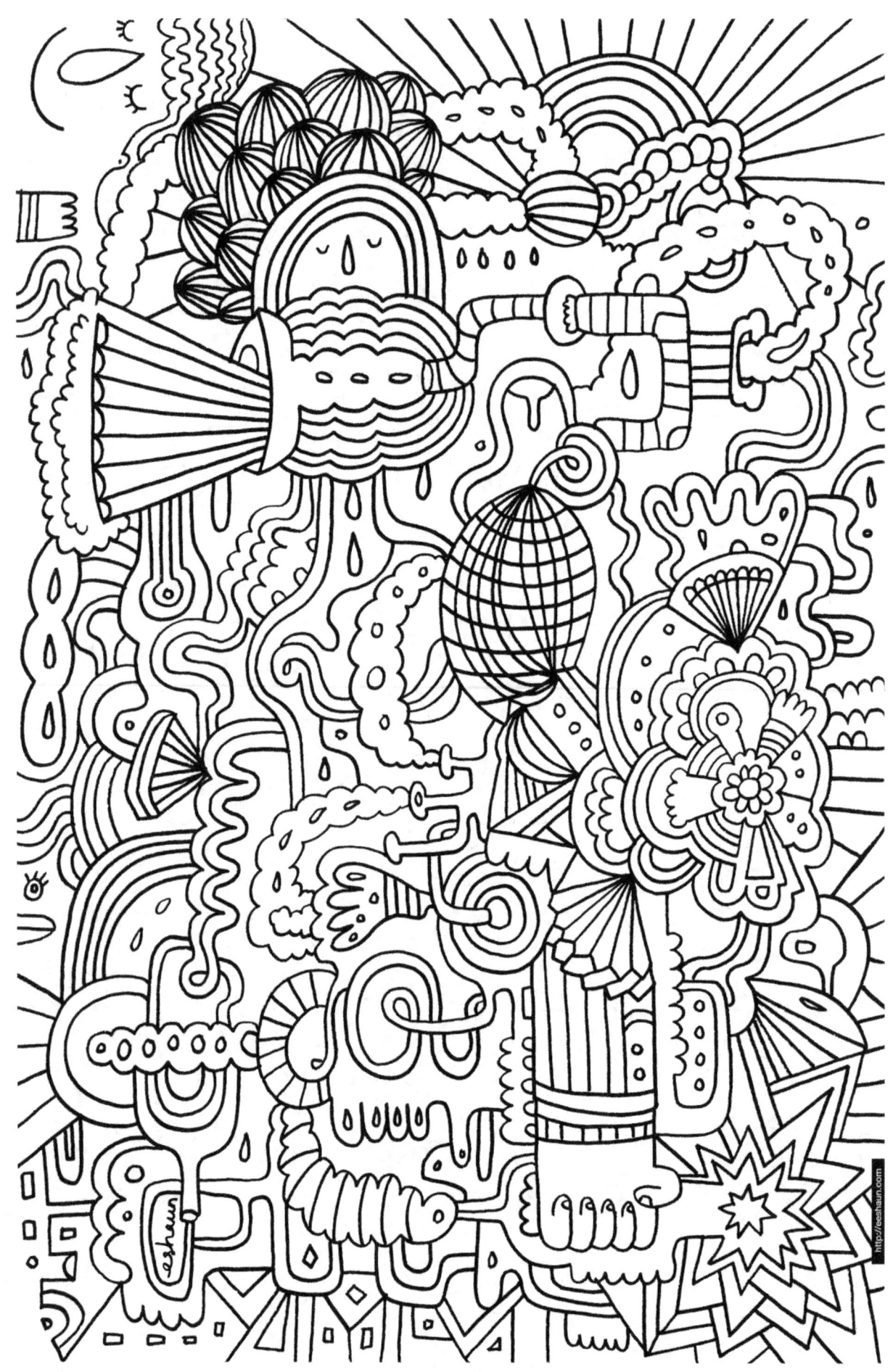

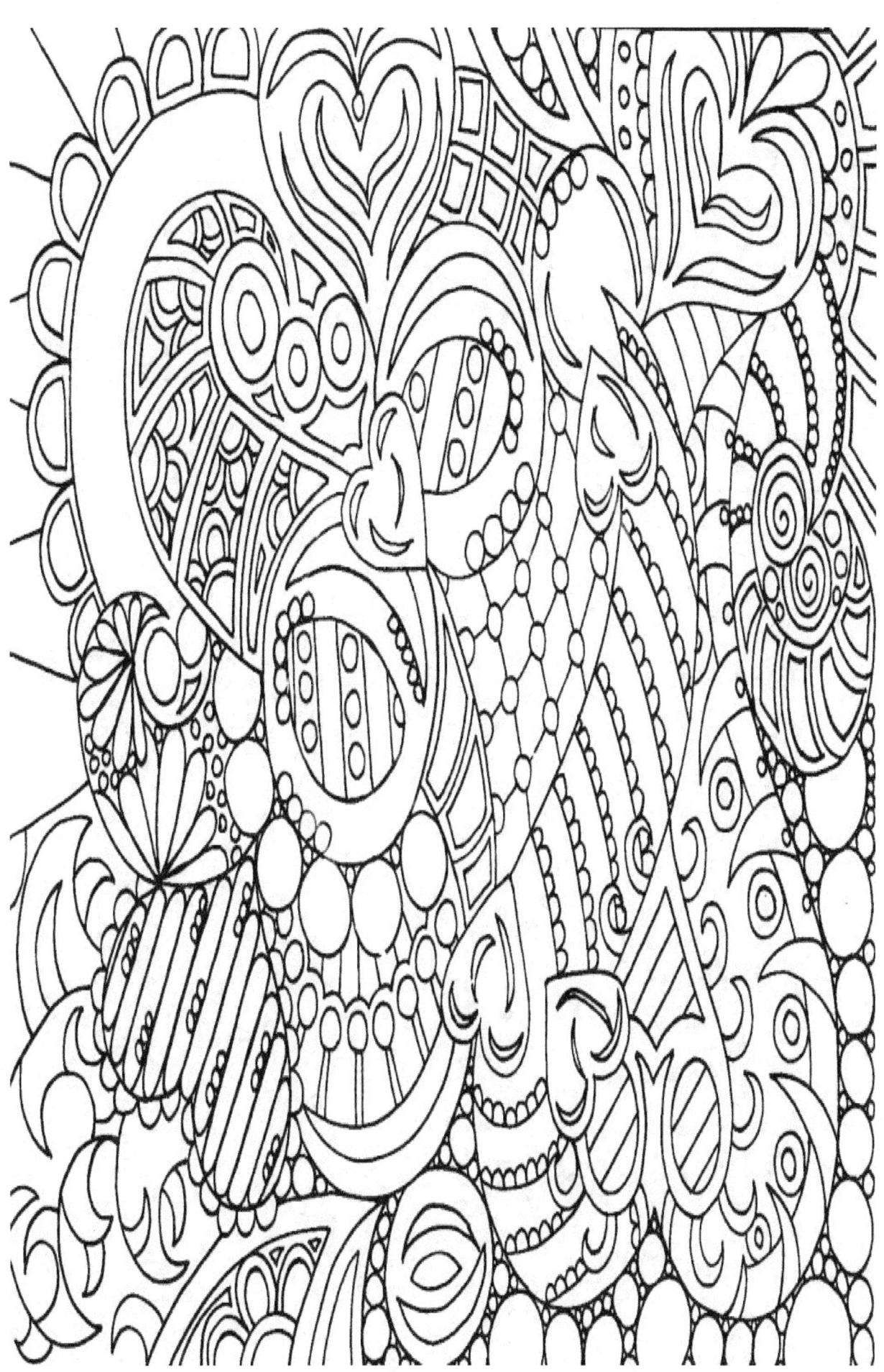

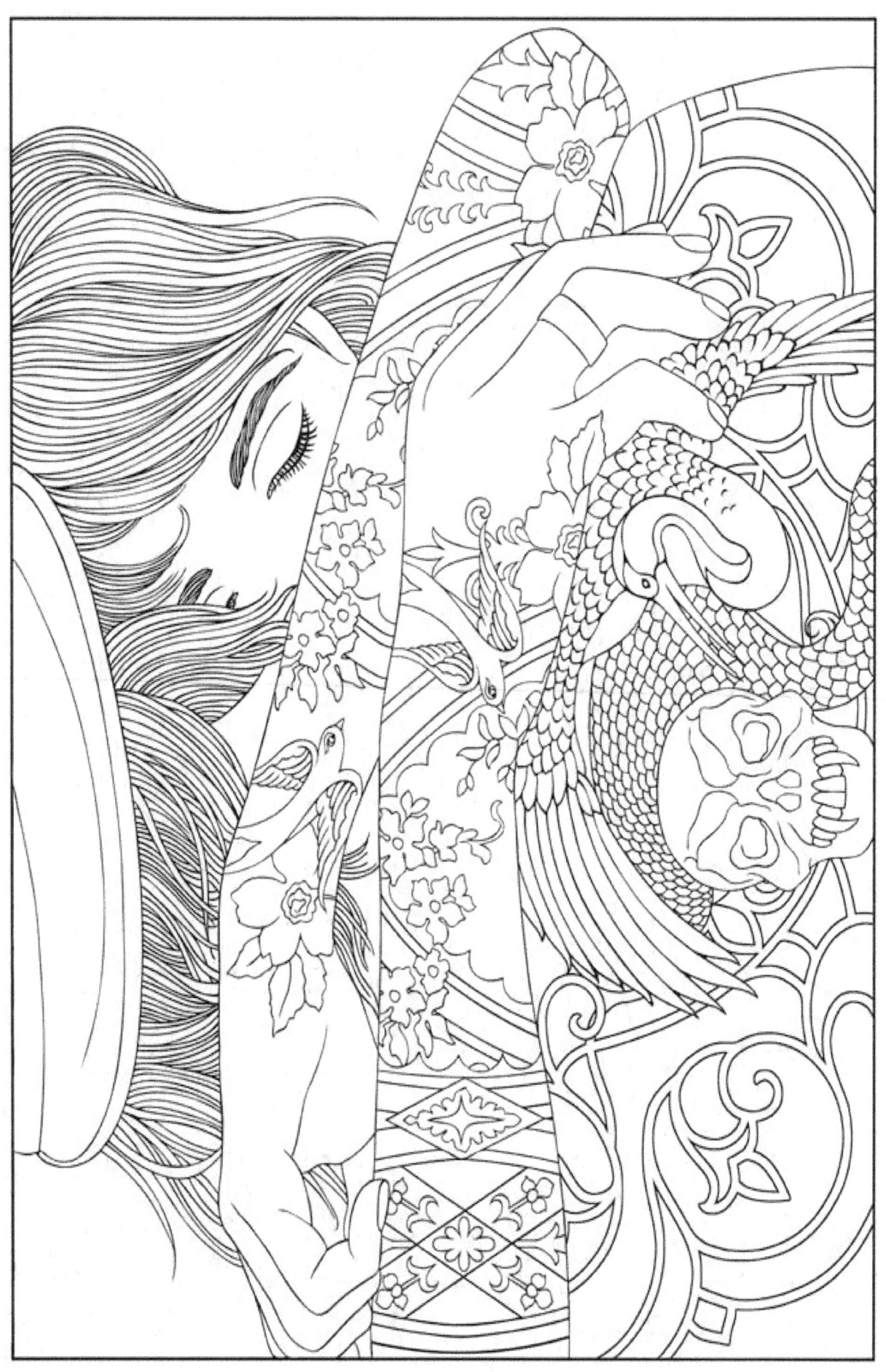

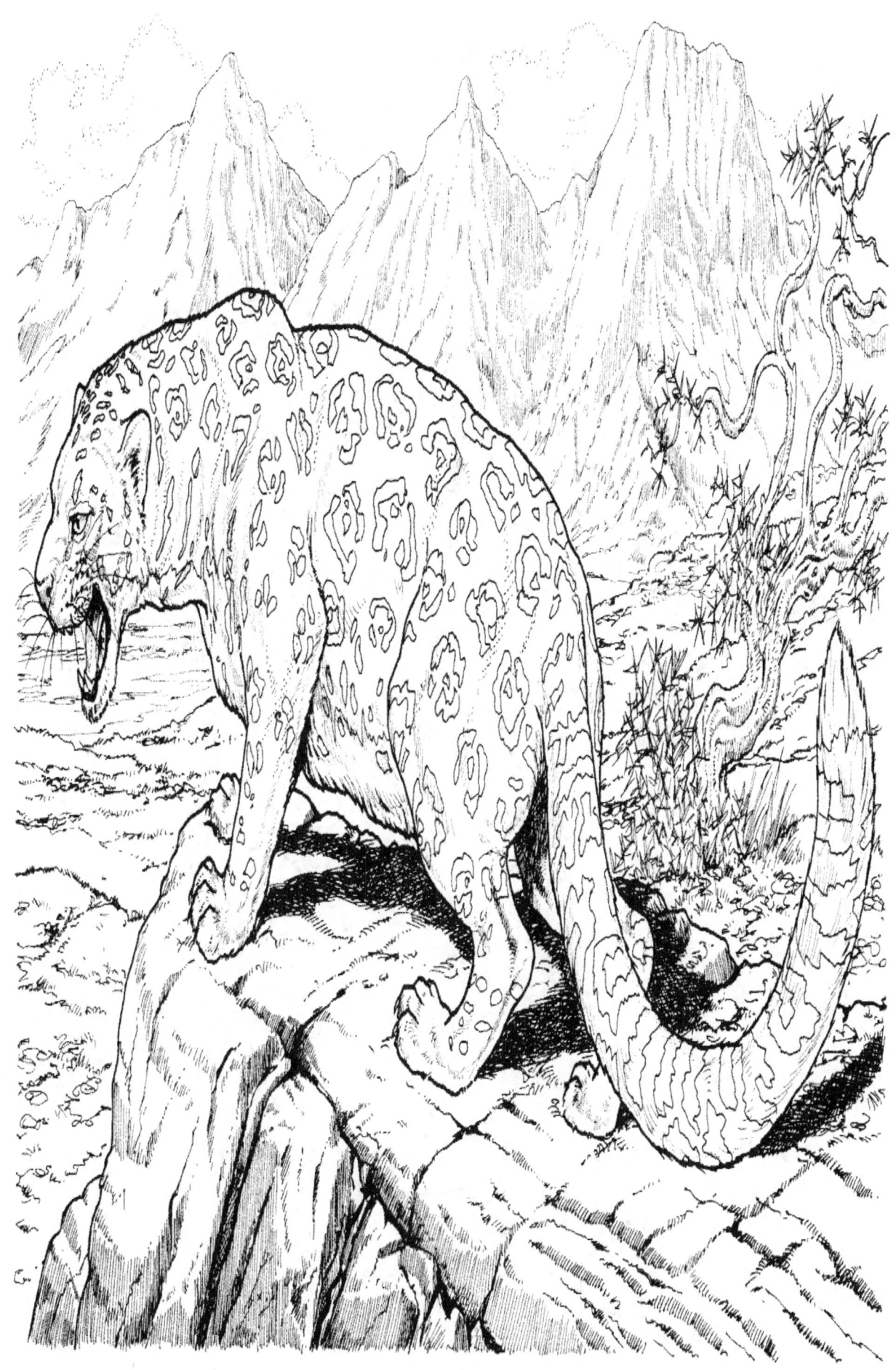

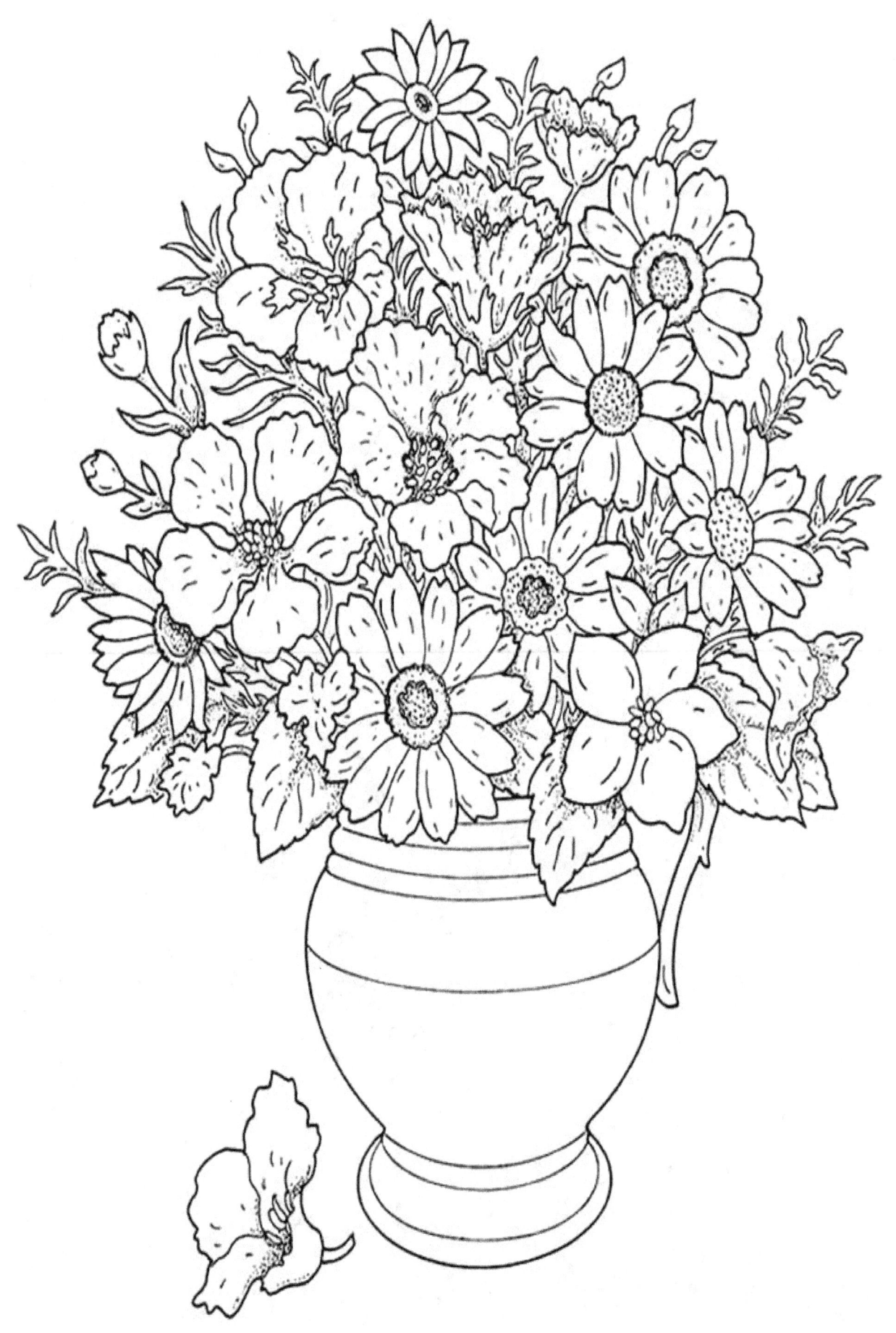

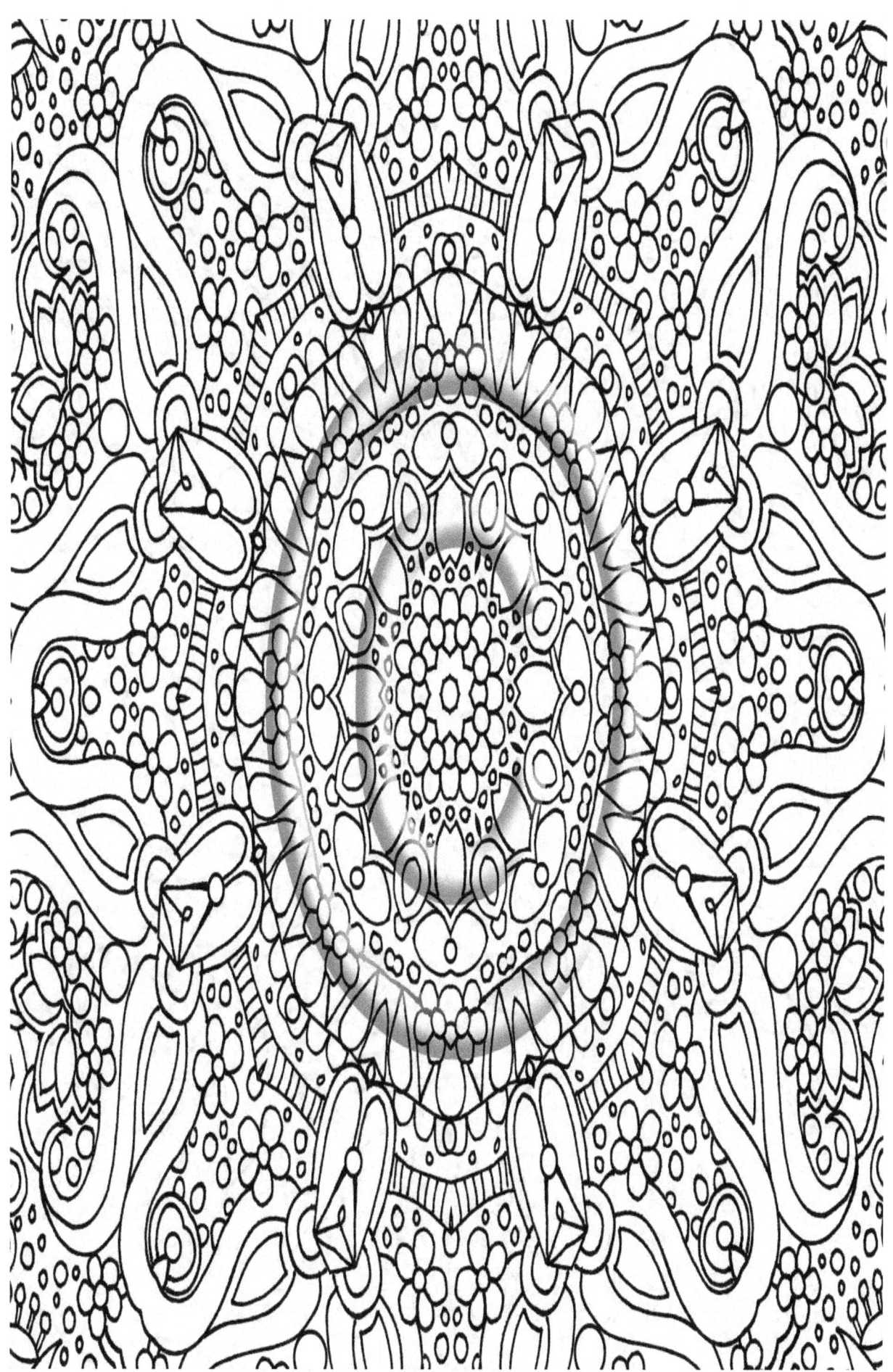

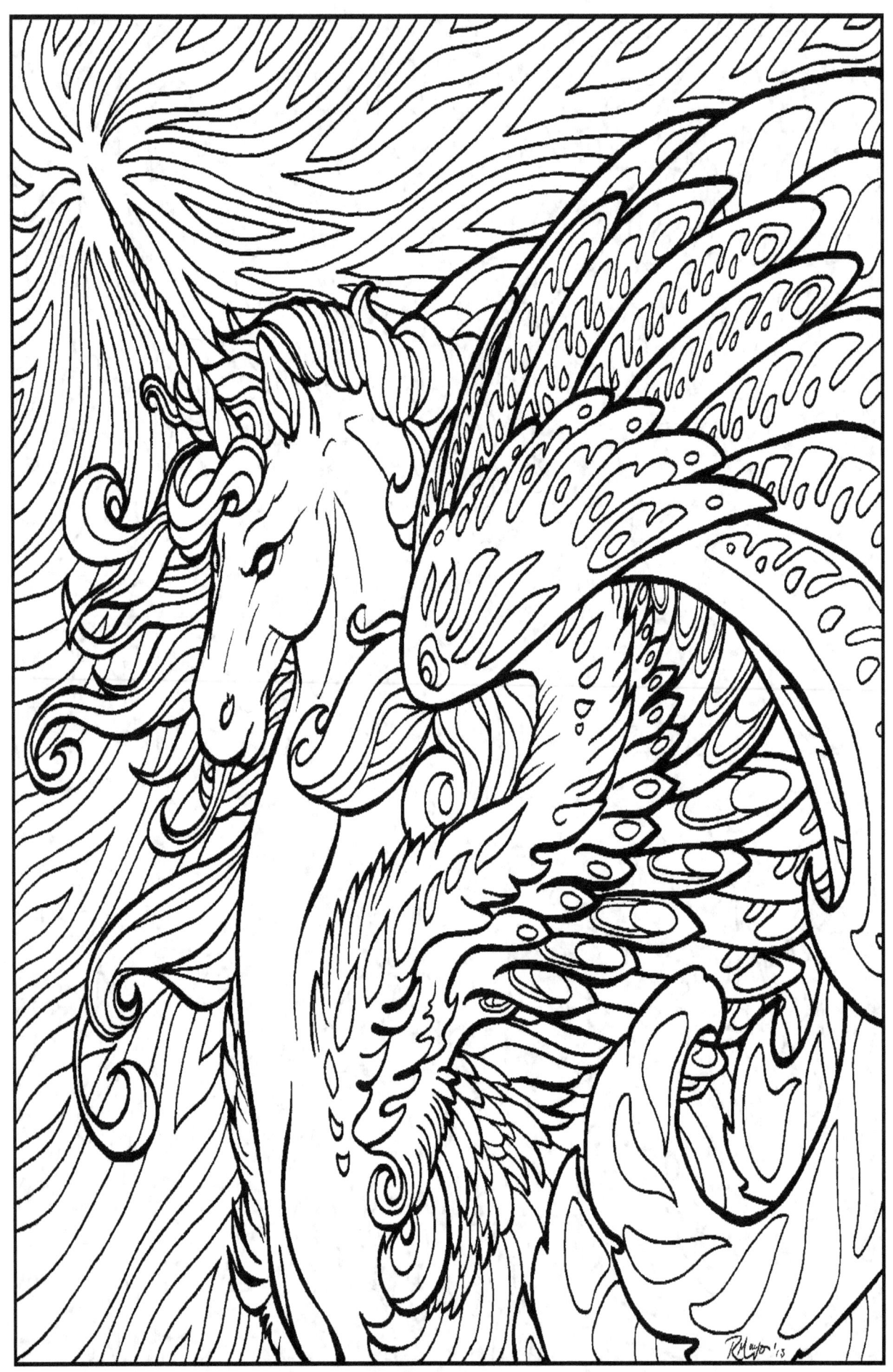

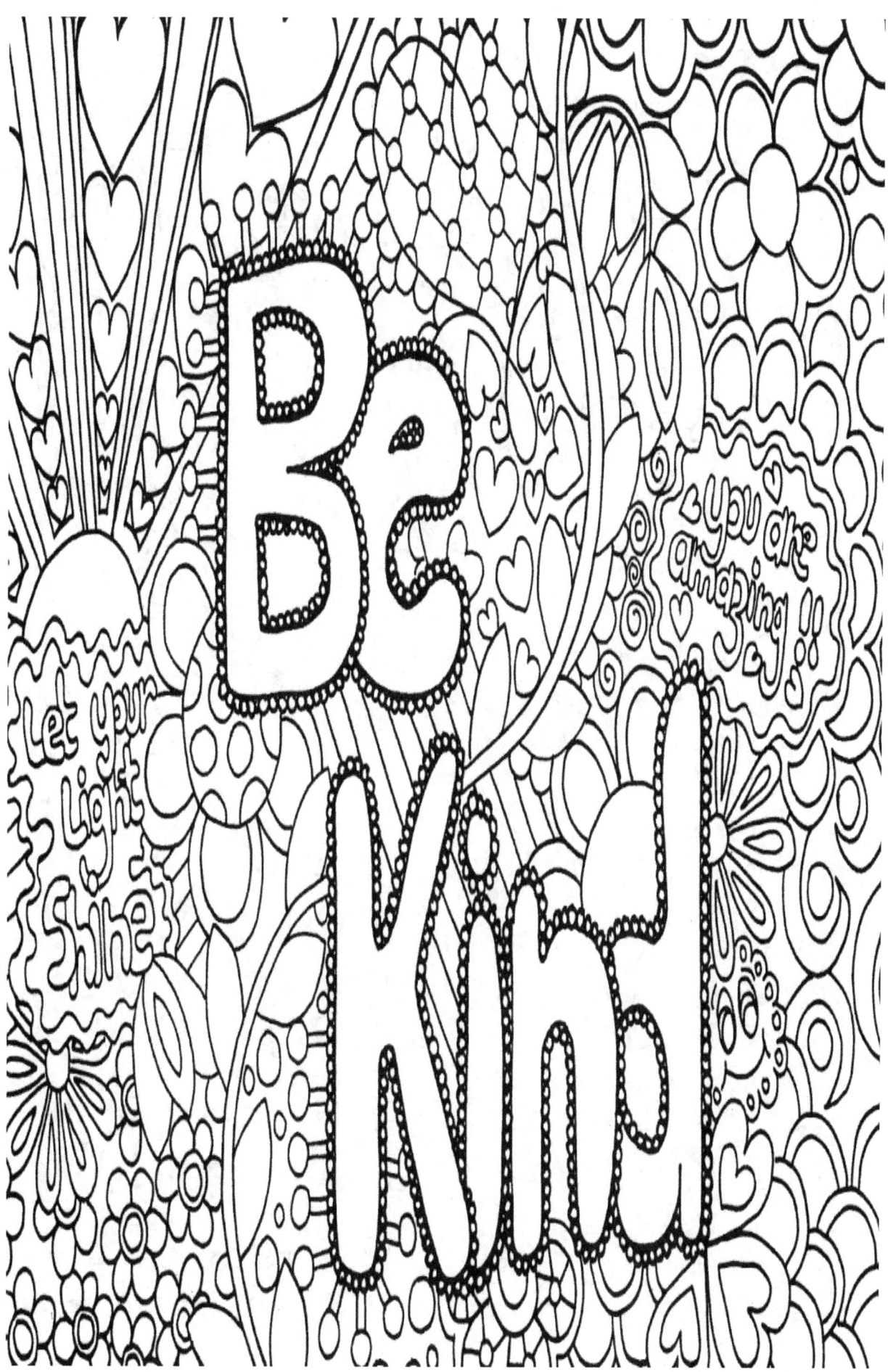

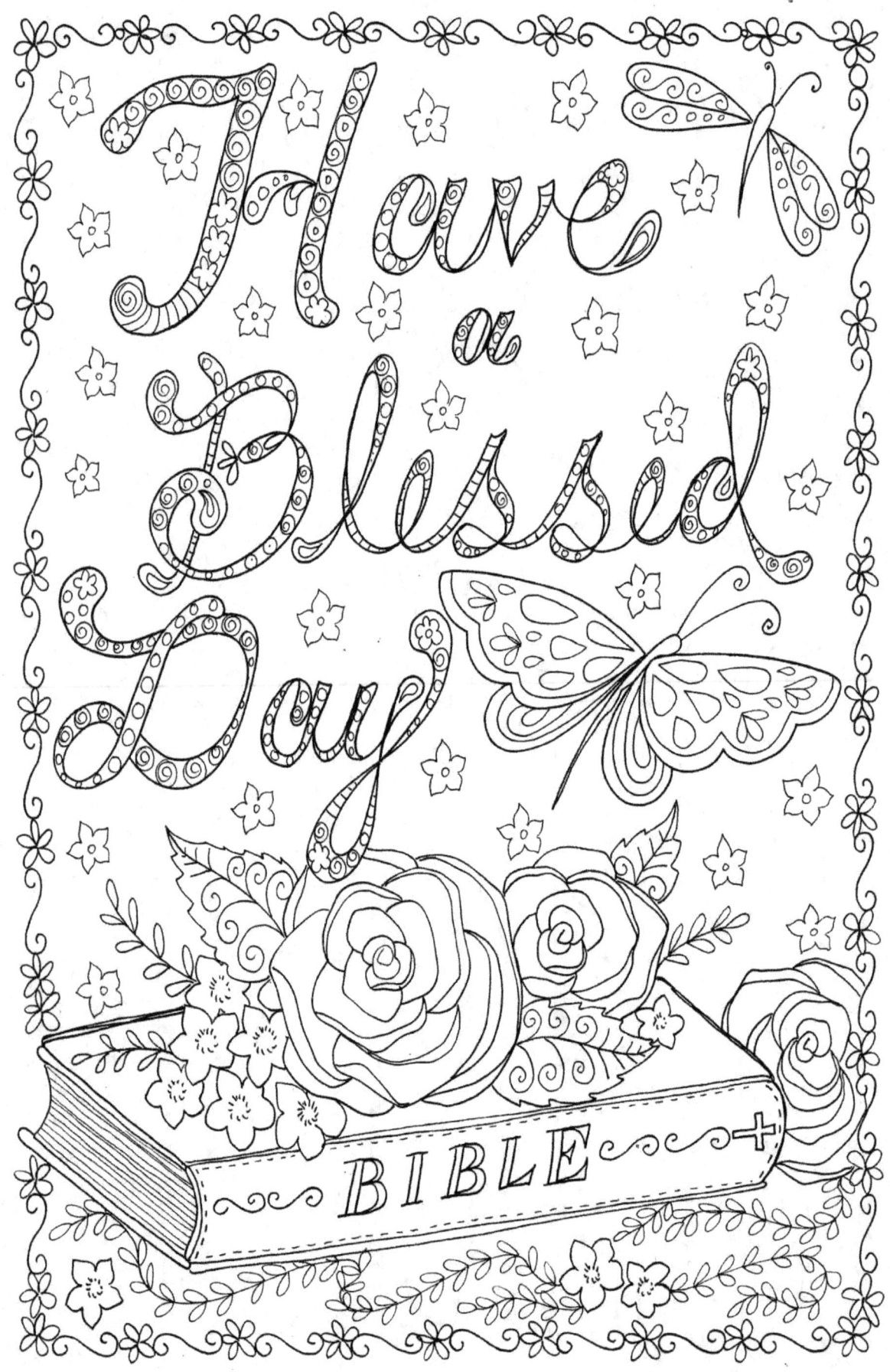

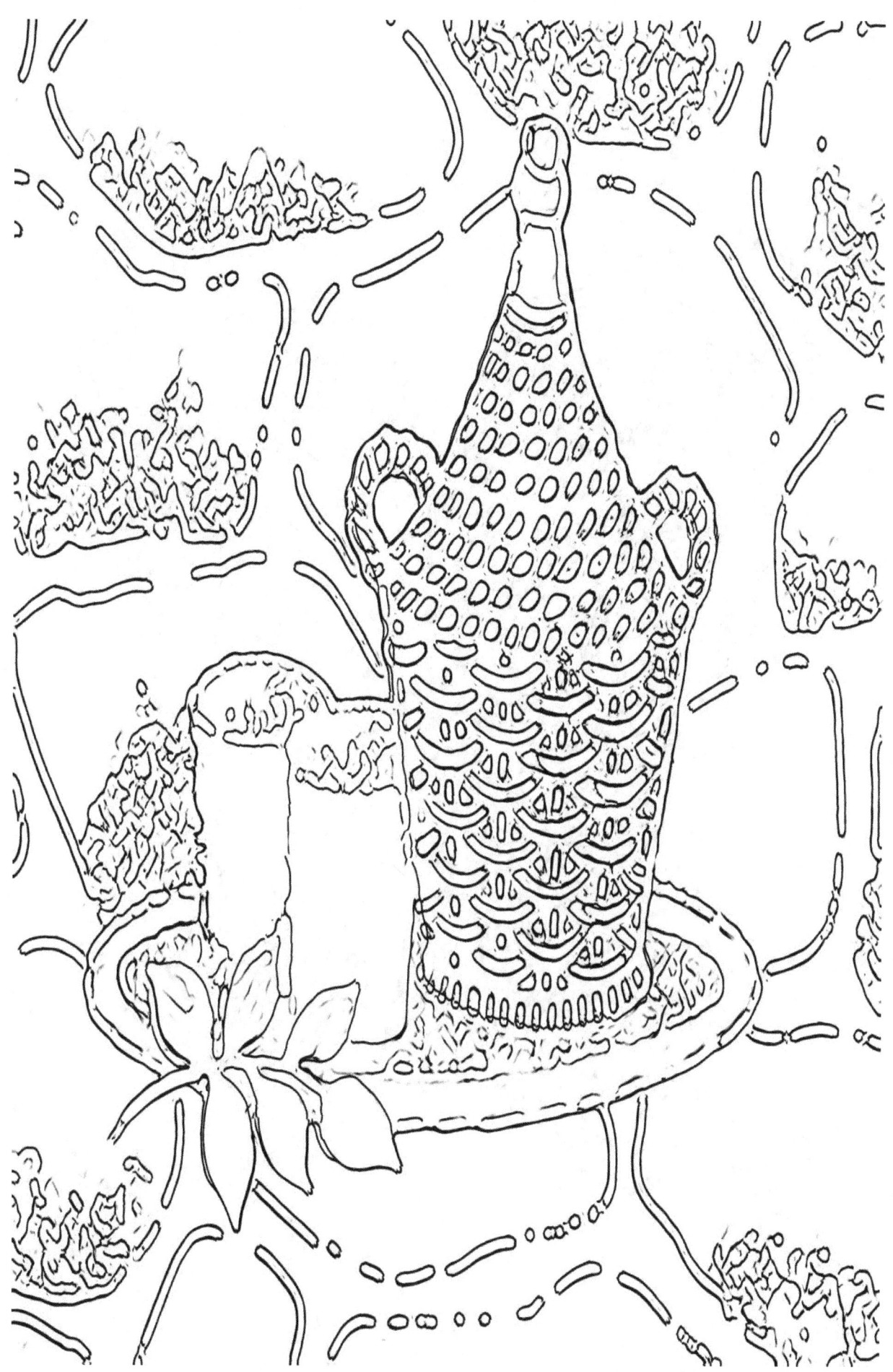

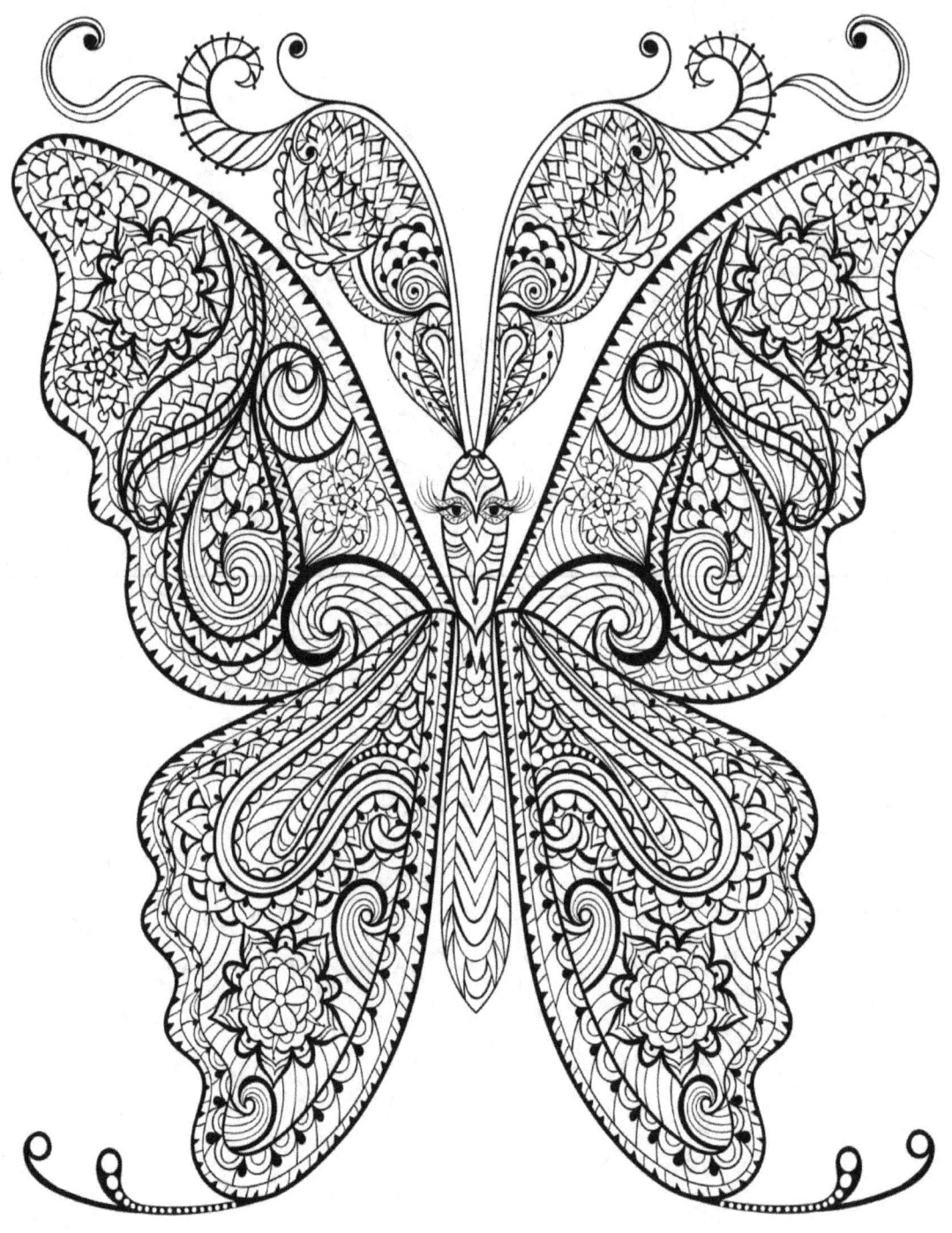

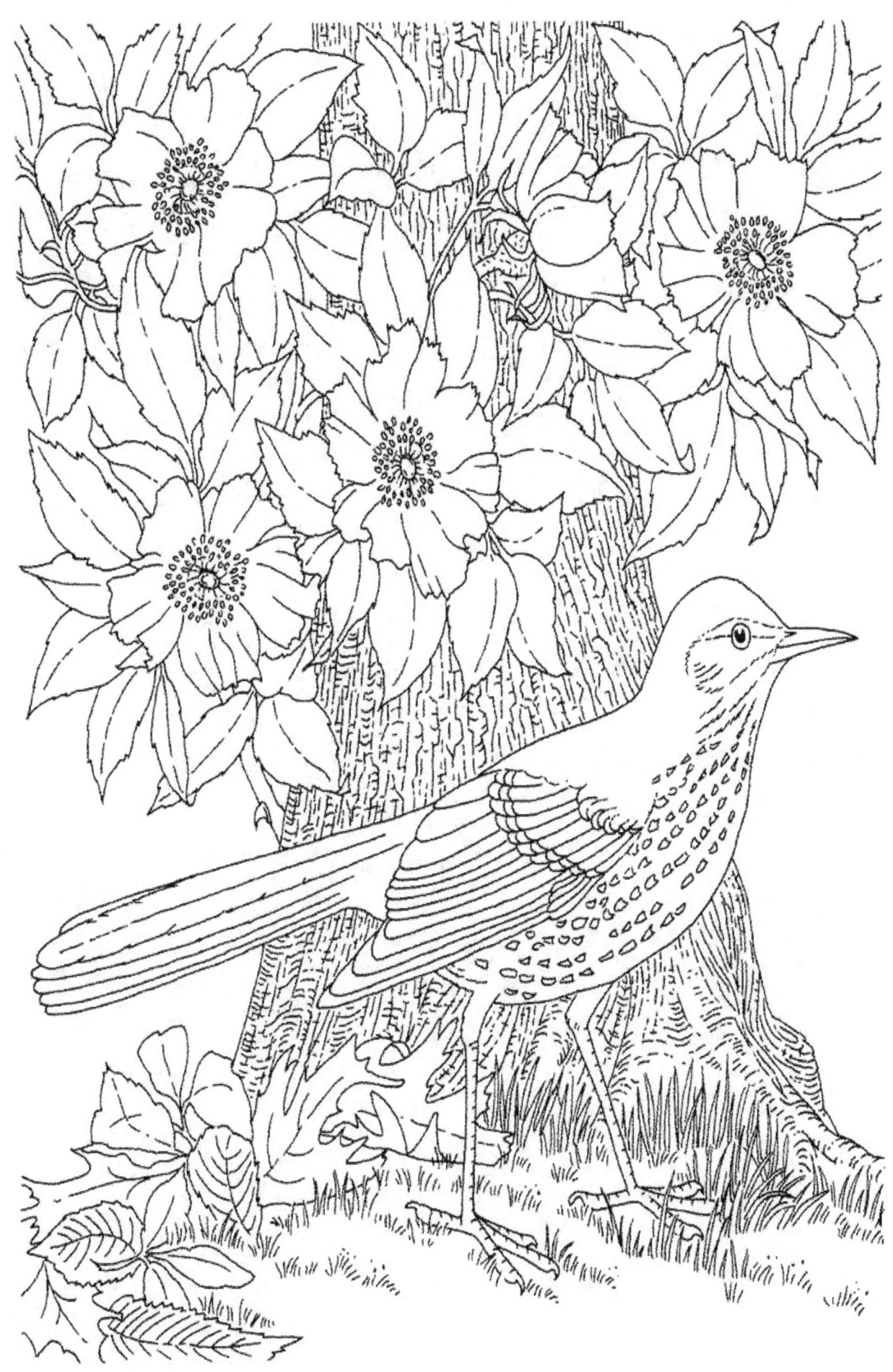

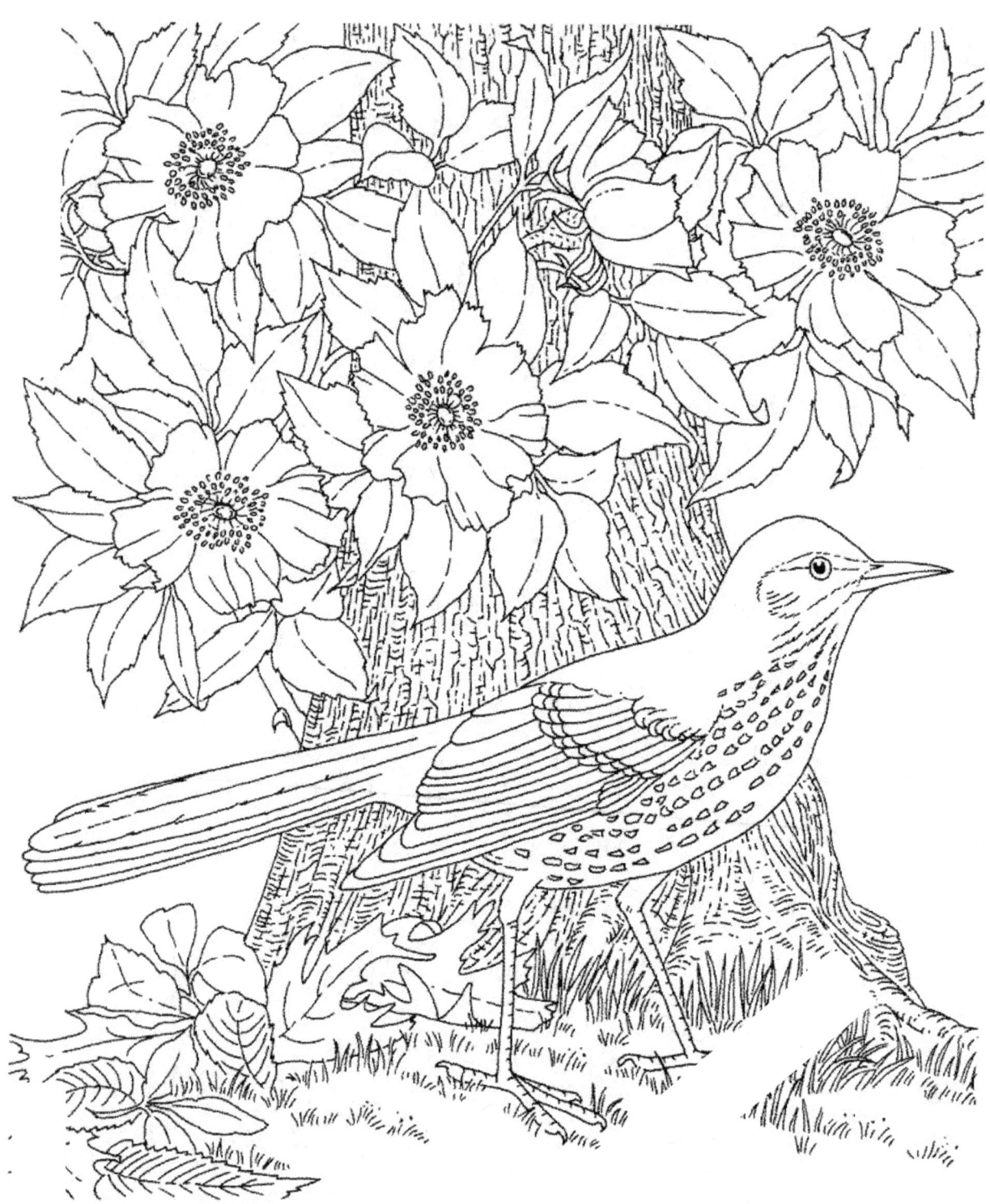

110214 Hops © EMERLYE ARTS

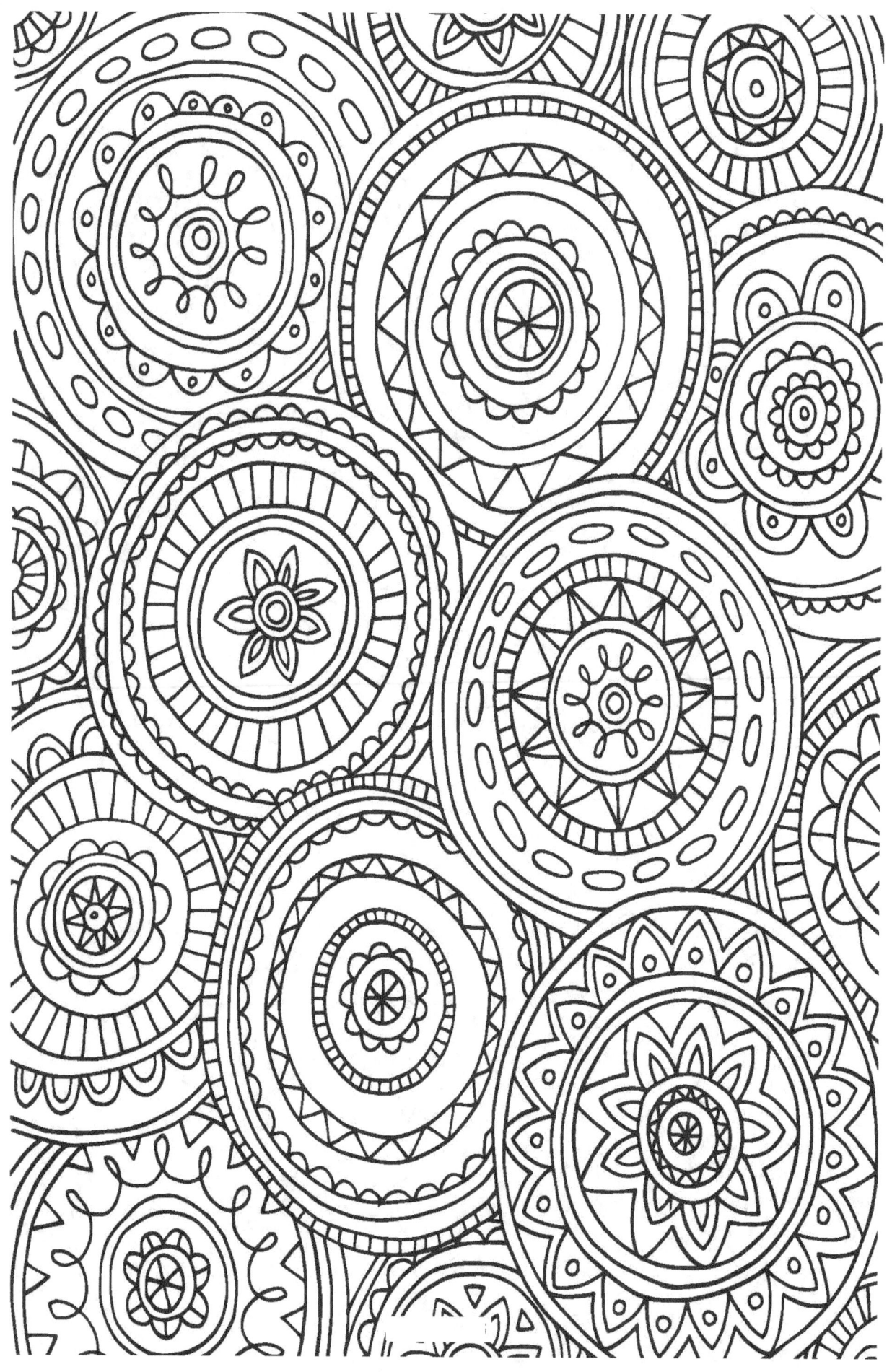

www.ingramcontent.com/pod-product-compliance
Lightning Source LLC
Chambersburg PA
CBHW062331220526
45469CB00008B/2661